BECOMING HER

Copyright © 2024 Laniece Herron

979-8-9911813-9-6

All rights reserved.

Notice: Neither the publisher nor the author is engaged in rendering professional advice or services to the individual reader. The ideas, procedures, and suggestions in this book are not intended as a substitute for consulting a licensed medical professional. All matters regarding your health require medical supervision. Neither the author nor the publisher shall be liable or responsible for any loss or damage allegedly arising from any information or suggestion in this book.

Herron, Laniece

Becoming Her: The Odyssey to Truth

Nonfiction / Memoir / Self-Help

Printed in the United States. No part of this publication may be reproduced, transmitted in any form or by any means, electronic or mechanical, including photocopying, recording, or any other information retrieval system, without the written permission of the publisher, except by a reviewer who may quote brief passages or reproduce illustrations in a review with the appropriate credits.

table of contents

	PROLOGUE	IX
INTRODUCTION:	The Journey Begins	11
CHAPTER 1:	I Am Her	17
CHAPTER 2:	Operating in the Un	31
CHAPTER 3:	Who Do You Love?	35
CHAPTER 4:	Breaking Up with Grace	45
CHAPTER 5:	Renewed Grace	51
CHAPTER 6:	Creating the Space	61
CHAPTER 7:	The Coupling	69
CHAPTER 8:	Moving Pots (Doing the Necessary Work)	73
CHAPTER 9:	Something on the Inside, Working on the Outside	79
CHAPTER 10:	Unforseeable	87
CHAPTER 11:	Unforgiveable	101
CHAPTER 12:	Loving from My Hurt Space	113

table of contents

CHAPTER 13:	Ungrateful	125
CHAPTER 14:	Unspoken	133
CHAPTER 15:	Forgiven	145
CHAPTER 16:	It Could Be Your Mother (Building Intentional Relationships)	153
CHAPTER 17:	Safety over Softness (Creating A Secure Life)	159
CHAPTER 18:	Loops and Lines (Breaking the Cycles and Setting the Boundaries)	163
CHAPTER 19:	Building Self-confidence	173
CHAPTER 20:	Awareness	183
CHAPTER 21:	Choose to Be Seen	187
	EPILOGUE	193
	AUTHOR'S NOTE	197

prologue

IMAGINE BEING A SEED, CAST INTO THE darkness of the soil in the most beautiful flowerpot. At first, it feels like an end, but it is, in fact, a profound beginning. Beneath the surface, away from the world's gaze, something miraculous happens. Roots unfurl, reaching down into the depths, anchoring you firmly. These roots—your foundation—are vital. They soak up the nutrients, the wisdom, the strength needed to transform potential into reality.

This period of being buried is not a time of inactivity but one of intense preparation. It is in this hidden phase that you gather the courage, the knowledge, and the resilience to push through the soil. And then, one day, you emerge. You break through the darkness into the light, stretching upwards, always following the sun—until the day when you're too big for your shiny new pot.

What happens when we outgrow the life we have? The life we're used to?

If you're not replanted, your growth could stunt. If you're not careful, your roots may become too exposed to the environment.

The sunflower's journey mirrors our own. The sun it follows is more than just a celestial body; it symbolizes the light within each of us. As the sunflower turns its face towards the sun, we too must turn inward, finding and nurturing the brilliance that resides in our souls.

And, we must also recognize when we're not growing anymore.

introduction
The Journey Begins

"Laniece, we are going to have to deliver. Your fever is spiking. If we don't, you will all die."

"If my babies have to go, so will I."

On August 2, 2014, I died.
Not literally, but spiritually.

I COULD NOT HAVE EXPERIENCED WHAT I had undergone and stayed the same. Death, of any kind, has a way of changing you.

The day we lost our twins was the day every internal wall I ever built was fractured beyond repair. Walls are built to protect, to keep out any danger and unwelcome weather or guest. It wasn't until after we lost the twins that I begin to see what I was protecting behind those walls—the very things that kept me feeling small and inadequate.

Little did I know the typhoon of pain, hurt, shame, and fear that lay behind those walls would burst open like a floodgate. There was an emotional tidal wave that would rupture my life and change who I was forever.

But before we enter our collective storms together, I want to celebrate you.

Why, you may be wondering. Because *Becoming Her* chooses you. This could mean a myriad of things, although I don't believe in coincidence.

You may think you chose this book; however, this type of material really decides who is searching for it and if they are ready to receive it. There is an awakening on the arising and parts of you must die for you to begin flourishing. It is a great reawakening, a pruning of sorts.

To be holding this book now, you are likely unapologetically at a point in life where you must have proven ready for something different. You might have specific changes in mind, or you may not know exactly where to start. Nevertheless, one thing is certain: There has to be more.

Speaking from personal experience, I know the feeling. I knew it even before losing the twins. For me, it was a constant nagging inside, a faint voice saying there is more to life than what you are settling for.

What is more? I wondered. *How am I settling?*

I think the suckiest part about growth is that no one can tell you all the decisions to make so you get it right.

(At least for me that is true.) I didn't want to get it wrong. I so badly desired for someone to tell me what to do and how to do it so that if there was a mistake, it wasn't mine… It wasn't on me.

I lacked belief in myself, so I put the pen of my life in others' hands so they could narrate my story. Accountability was so far from my vocabulary that I was willing to give my power to anyone I thought may have the answers, anyone who might take the bait if things turned out wrong or went awry.

If I'm honest, the only thing standing in the way between me and this "more to life" was me. And the same goes for you. I had created my own personal prison that kept me close enough to see change on the horizon but far enough that I felt safe from having to travel the unknown to reach it. That prison foundation was built on fear. My fears were so debilitating that I accepted less from myself and others. And I want you to understand that when you live like this for long enough, it feels normal. You still have days that may be full of laughter and fun. You can also still accomplish a lot of goals and on the outside look like you have it all together. But inside, you're carrying this dirty little secret: I am not enough.

AS CHILDREN, WE PLAYED Hide and Seek. One person counts to twenty while all the kids are scattered throughout the neighborhood. The seeker could be looking for their friends for several blocks, finding them in all types of places. And, let's be honest. There's always one person for whom, when after a certain amount of time and searching, you call it quits.

As adults, I feel like we are still playing this game but on a deeper level. We live our lives, putting up facades, trying our best to save face while losing connection to who we really are. So many people fear embarrassment because of the validation they seek from others.

And what happens because of that? We never try, or we won't try things that will attract any type of "negative" attention.

Honestly, to some degree, we've all become that kid who went so far that no one decided to look for and called quits on ourselves. In those instances, we willingly give our pens away.

This book is about taking that pen back. *Becoming Her* is written to remind you that you're the main freaking character and the narrator of your own story. You rock!

You, my dear, are a *star!*

Yes, I will be sharing with you some of my story with hopes that you see yourself in parts of it. However, pull from the pieces that honor the space and time you are in then find the courage to begin trusting in yourself again. My hope is that you can use some of the many tools I have found and begin writing your story from a place of power, a place of healing, a place of freedom!

Why?

Because, for me, becoming isn't about arriving somewhere or achieving a certain aim anymore. It is, instead, a forward motion—a means of evolving, a way to reach continuously toward a better self. The journey doesn't end. (Paraphrasing Michelle Obama) And I pray *Becoming Her* inspires you to turn another page, to start another chapter, and to write freely from the depths of your soul.

This is only the beginning.

Write out loud.

chapter 1
I Am Her

"Freeing yourself was one thing, claiming ownership of that freed self was another."

—TONI MORRISON

I AM LANIECE—WIFE, MOTHER, AND veteran. I am also an educated professional, who holds a bachelors in administration and a masters in social work.

Blah blah blah blah...

The list of my accomplishments and accolades could go on and on. Still, it would not depict how empty and unfulfilled I felt for a significant period in my life. So, allow me to officially reintroduce myself, as there was not one accomplishment that includes my children making me feel whole.

Hello! I am Laniece—wife to Darnell, mother to Kennedy, Kaia, DJ, Darius, and Lennox. I am also a veteran in the

United States Air Force. I was taught to serve this country, but most importantly, I learned to serve my family as an extension of serving myself.

Now, that's better!

Grief is both humbling and transformational. It is the grenade that will explode and expose your very foundation. It was not until I was completely broken that I was able to do the work to heal and fully embrace every aspect of myself as a person, which includes being the mother of five.

Our healing and happiness can be aided by things outside of ourselves, but those external things will never be the root cause of our internal peace and joy. To begin to live a life reflective of the woman you are, you will need to go inward. I remember reading things like this statement before, thinking *how the heck do you go inward and who has time for that?* It felt ethereal and out of reach because I couldn't conceptualize it.

Funny thing about life is it will make time for you. And it is up to you what you do with your time. Will you use it to question God or the universe about why this shouldn't be happening to you, or will you use it to reflect and see the lessons that can be taken from the experience?

Don't get it twisted. Both are possible.

I still shift from "God, what the…" to "God, allow me to see what you're doing here," or "I know there is something amazing here for me." The difference in these reactions is simple: Choice.

Choice is something you get to exercise. The more you exercise it, the stronger it becomes. If you are constantly flexing this muscle to adjust to fear, struggle, or lack, then your choices will reflect that. But if you're exercising it to calibrate possibilities, opportunities, and growth, you will see a life reflective of that also.

In my experience in every corner of my life, I learned both visually and audibly that Black women have had to be strong forever, and I was not an exception to this rule. Culturally, it seems to be an initiation to becoming a woman and figuring how much we can handle before we break. And even in our breakdown, we "bet not" show a sign of letting up. That would be admitting weakness—not creating space for our own pleasures and desires, letting them be pushed *waaaaaaay* back.

Our light is covered by the cloak of responsibilities that have been handed down through generations from an early age. The additional bricks of expectations are placed upon us by our current roles that get cemented by the "not enoughness" we've seemingly carried through our childhood. What I am saying is it can all feel like too much. How are we supposed to let our essence shine through when we've lost touch and connection with what our own unique essence even means? How could I be a good wife and a good mother when I did not truly understand what it meant to be good to me?

I am going to say something, and y'all may not like it, but sexual trauma is more common than we ever like to speak of—so much hurt covered by humor and silent tears only shed when we are alone with our despair. Many of us learn, at a young age, that making a way out of no way is a necessary skill to survive, never asking for help because we should be able to handle it, and we don't want to ever owe anyone because, God forbid, they hold that over our head.

When I look back on my life, I feel like there was a point that resembles a constant whirlwind following me. I want to set the record straight before we move any further.

I am a quick runner, not the fastest but pretty quick; still, there was one person I could not seem to outrun, no matter the distance I tried to force between us and that was me. Having to deal with me and my emotions was not something I thought was necessary, and I did not see the value in it. Honestly, somewhere along the way, I adopted the belief that being strong meant always putting on a good face. In my culture, perhaps even my community, this is a given. There was no time for tears or breakdowns because I needed to be able to push through. So, in typical denial, I avoided it. I suppressed all those emotions and feelings I had about myself that developed over time through different life experiences.

I would rather pretend and move as if they didn't happen or as if they didn't have an impact on me than to deal with them.

Another funny thing about life is that whatever lesson you don't learn, it will find its way back to you as many times as necessary. There is no hole or cave deep and dark enough for you to push the unwanted feelings, memories, and emotions needed to learn from into that they can't seep their way out. *Trust me, I've tried.*

Some could say I grew up fast, but others may suggest my maturity was lacking in certain areas. Either way, everything that has happened in my life prepared me to become the person I am. It took me some time to recognize that, but once I was aware, I became unstoppable. The same is true for you. Once you recognize your life experiences have only aided you into becoming the powerful person you are, you will begin to feel equally unstoppable—not because nothing bad will ever happen again, but because you know there is nothing that can happen you can't use to learn and grow from.

The change we are working on is happening from the inside and shining on the outside. Once you begin to change what's happening on your inside, the outside will become your wildest dreams. This is your odyssey—the journey that does not stop.

You will always find ways to learn and receive the lessons that come your way if you are open and receptive to them. This may seem like a lot, and it was something I had struggles with myself (because my beliefs and daily practices had me believing I knew it all and no one could tell me any different, especially about me). How I approached the world and situations was rooted in ignorance and that ignorance only caused me undue pain and misery. If you don't like where you are and you want to be somewhere different, then you must learn to be okay with not knowing…with accepting yourself where you are so that you can begin to learn and grow to get to the place you were destined to be.

It is important to learn how to practice humility because pride will leave you stuck. Sooooo, can you do that? Can you begin to check your pride at the door? And I am talking every door—wife door, girlfriend door, sister door, coworker door, mother door, etc. I want you to remember we are all learning daily. No one (and I mean no one) has all the answers, but there are a lot of people who have found peace. And they have found this peace through introspection, accountability, flexibility, adaptability, and daily practice—something I know a lot about.

We all experience pain differently, and I have experienced a fair amount in my life. But what I am about to share altered me and my reality forever.

In 2014, my husband, Darnell, and I had been married for three years. We were both active-duty Air Force and had recently relocated to Alaska with our beautiful baby girl, who at the time had just turned three. He and I started talking about having another baby, no real planning just talks. But for me, that's all that needs to happen—talking. I inherited my mother's ability to reproduce with no issue, something like a Fertile Myrtle. *So, voila!* Within the month of talking about it, I was pregnant.

We set up our first ultrasound appointment and were super excited! It just so happened to be April 1st. I remember the doctor having a confused look on her face as she conducted my sonogram, which caused me to worry. Then she left the office to get another doctor. As the second one verified what the first had seen, they announced we were having twins! My husband and I were in complete shock and just knew this was an April Fool's joke because no one in our families had ever had twins. We were ecstatic, to say the least! We told our closest family and friends but decided to keep it to ourselves until we made it into our second trimester. Then, just after hitting twenty weeks—in typical millennial style—I shared a Facebook post, announcing to the world that we were having twins. I even made custom shirts; it was the cutest heartfelt post.

With all the budding excitement surrounding the births of our babies, July 30, 2014 will forever be a day etched into my memory. I was twenty-two weeks pregnant with our daughter and son, and tired was an understatement. This particular morning was no different from any other Wednesday morning. I remember getting ready for Physical Training (PT); remember, I am in the military. After getting myself together, I got our daughter ready for daycare, feeling particularly good that morning. After I dropped her off, I headed to the gym. Although I was limited by what I could do in my workout, I still had to participate as much as possible. So, I did what I could and afterwards felt fine.

Once I got back home, I showered and got ready for work. When I arrived, I sat down and began to carry on with my daily duties. I started to feel some pain in my stomach, but I tried to brush it off. As the pain increased, I walked into the office and told my supervisor I was going to the hospital because something did not feel right. He asked, "Who's out there to cover you?" I began to get upset and said, "I'm leaving." He then stated, "Well, you know if you had those babies now that'd be bad." The look I gave him devoured his entire soul, and I walked out of there no longer looking for permission.

I left work frustrated because he was stalling me, and I knew I had to get to the hospital. I called my husband, and he met me at our house and drove me there. We lived a good forty-five minutes away from the military hospital, so I prayed while my husband reassured me everything would be fine. When we arrived, the doctor did a routine checkup in Labor and Delivery. It wasn't until she checked me with those metal prongs that she could see my sac had prolapsed into the vaginal area. Not knowing what damage she may have caused by sticking the prongs in, she removed them, and I was admitted immediately. That's when my contractions began coming back-to-back. Everything was moving so fast; they were trying to put an IV in and stuck me about seven times. My husband screamed at the tech to stop because I was in so much pain. He was protecting me and our babies at all costs.

They finally got a nurse in who could do the IV without killing me. The uncertainty and panic in the air was so thick, you could slice it with a knife. The medical staff all seemed so unsure of what to do but finally gave me some medicine to stop the contractions. For the first time that day I felt like everything was going to be okay.

Soon my doctor came in and told us, "You know, at this point the twins are not viable. You need to make it to twenty-three weeks for us to be able to do anything." The way she said it—with no compassion or an ounce of understanding—I was crushed. My parents prayed. My friends prayed. We were just hoping for the best.

After four days of being inverted in bed—trying to keep my babies in—I woke up, and I told my husband, "Happy Anniversary." As the day proceeded, I developed a fever. When my doctor entered, I felt the temperature lower as she brought an unwelcoming chill with her. This part is a blur, but I do recall her being cold and stoic as she delivered the news that they would be inducing me. What she said already hurt, but how she said it in her militant stance and voice was like an ice dagger to my heart.

Either me, my sister-friend who visited, or my husband said something. She was told that her behavior in my presence was unacceptable because it made my already painful position feel that much more impossible. My doctor had a fear in her eyes I knew all too well. The ice began to melt, and she cried. And there it was: Hopelessness. The truth didn't need to be spoken; she felt just as helpless as I did, but she had to make a decision and so did I.

Devastated, I looked to my husband and my close friend to see if they could help me. I needed someone to save me after the doctor had said "if I didn't deliver, we would all die"—me and both my babies.

My husband said, "We can have more babies, Baby. There is only one you."

"I'd rather die with my babies," I responded.

I was not ready to let go. I hadn't even considered my daughter at that moment and began to pray something fierce. I had to believe there was a divine purpose behind all the pain.

I was tired and it felt like no decision was a good one. The room felt like it was spinning, and I helplessly wanted someone else to decide. All I wanted to know was why me.

After deliberating for what felt like hours, I finally let go and said, "If God wants my babies, He can have them." And in that moment, I felt like God had removed me from my body. I was there, but I wasn't. An insane amount of peace had poured over me, and it was truly an outer-body experience.

I believe that was the first time in my then twenty-four years of living that I wholly felt and accepted God's love—that unconditional, merciful, all-knowing love. I had to surrender because there was only so much my human mind could comprehend and handle. My mental state had become as fragile as the first layer of ice on a calm lake on a frigid winter morning. Any missed steps could have sunk me deeper into the depths of despair.

Before God covered me that day, everything around me moved in slow motion. What probably took hours felt like an eternity. My sense of time was altered, reality shifted. It was like as soon as I was about to break, God wrapped me in His arms mentally, physically, emotionally, and spiritually. He said, "I got you."

On August 2, 2014, at twenty-two weeks pregnant, I gave birth to two beautiful angels. I delivered our daughter first and they laid her on my chest. She looked just like her sister; I could not bear it. I had them take her and next came our son. He was bigger and so handsome, but I did not hold him at all. I couldn't. I simply watched. They were alive for two hours before taking their last breath.

After it was all said and done, all I wanted to do was feel nothing at all. The hospital staff told me I could have anything, and I said, "All I want is something to make me numb." They put me out. When I woke up the babies were gone, and they still had the beds out with all the blood on them. I began to scream, "Take them out of here!"

They told me anytime I wanted to see the babies I could, so the next day I braced myself to say my final goodbye. A nurse went down and came back. She said there had been a mistake; my babies were taken to the morgue already. I felt like I lost them all over again—hardest four days of my life.

We did get to go into the morgue, and I read them my favorite childhood book, *The Giving Tree* by Shel Silverstein. I kissed them and rubbed their hands, assuring them that Mommy would be there with them one day. As we said our final goodbyes, I felt a piece of me stay in that room with them.

This was the beginning of the fracture to my already fragile reality. I could no longer suffer in silence because the pain I experienced was not just from losing the twins but from everything I had stuffed down and away, because I did not want to deal with it as a result of the shame and guilt it all held. I didn't want to know that Laniece or even look at her.

That Laniece deserved to lose her babies.

That Laniece was unworthy of anything good and suffering should be her lifelong companion.

That was my narrative, my constant reminder that I wasn't good enough—that I wasn't worthy. I'd tried for twenty-four years to bury that Laniece, and I had done an amazing job of ridding myself of her until then. People would often describe me as fun-loving, funny, a light, and just a genuinely good person to be around. But there was a deep darkness and a sadness to me I never shared or showed anyone. There was a time when I would periodically stare blankly into the mirror at myself, reinforcing how damaged I was and criticizing every inch of my being. She showed up. She came back, this time with a vengeance.

I joined the Air Force to get away from her. To go to a place where no one knew her, a place where I could create a new narrative—one that did not include the baggage I so desperately wanted to leave behind. And that's exactly what I did. I moved pots and kept my soil. (I'll explain later.)

There's a belief I hold, and it may not resonate with you. Even though I held such deep-rooted beliefs about myself, there were blessings all around me *for me*. The belief is that everything is lined up for me; everything I could ever hope or pray for is waiting for me to be in alignment. And sometimes even when I am not fully in alignment (like, maybe I made it there by mistake), blessings find their way to me. That is the belief—my belief. But when "blessings" happen under these circumstances, I am not always a good steward of them. I don't value the worth of them because I am struggling with the worth within myself, the idea that they are mine.

During this time, I was blessed to have a husband, and we had a beautiful daughter. But the darkness of losing the twins never left me. I could feel it seep through daily. Some days were better than others, but it was always lurking in the shadows, patiently waiting for the moment it could overcome me—the moment where I would feel weighed down and turn to anger and coldness. No one was exempt from the coldness and anger, and writing those words brings tears to my eyes because I am a mom. I know my daughter felt it, no matter how hard I tried to hide it. I was patching my holes and after the loss of the twins that wasn't even an option. I was in pieces.

chapter 2
Operating in the Un

"When you love and accept yourself, when you know who really cares about you, and when you learn from your mistakes, then you stop caring about what people who don't know you think."

—BEYONCÉ KNOWLES

NOT ONLY WAS I SETTLING BUT ADD suffering to it. The loss of my babies took a toll on me I wasn't prepared to pay. Therefore, this chapter is dedicated to every lie the world sold me that I willingly bought. For such a long time, I deemed myself as unworthy. To be unworthy, as deemed by Oxford Languages, means to not be deserving of respect or attention. But how could I not be worthy of being a mother?

Hear me! When your self-esteem is low, it will manifest in all areas of your life—most likely, ending with you not making the best or most worthy decisions for yourself. With that unworthiness, we enter into an avalanche of uns:

*Un*certain, *un*able, *un*important. (You get the picture.) But the uns that had gained control of my motherboard were unlovable, unforgivable, and unseen.

The prefix "un" means not. To go throughout your days believing, at your core, you are not worthy or that you are not loveable—particularly as a child—has a profound impact on the way you view yourself and others. It has a profound impact on how you interact with yourself and others, too. It can and will hold you back from the most precious love you can experience in this life—the love you give and show yourself. I call it "Operating in the Un," which is operating from a place of scarcity, the place of not enoughness. I know I am not the only person who has felt this. I also know there is a way to drop the *un*.

It's time to drop the uns in your life, too. They are prefixes you've willingly accepted until now.

Nothing is "un" until you say it is. And you may not choose to say you're "un" anything, but your actions may be screaming it. Because what you believe will always outweigh what you say. Either way, I am here to help you fall in love with you—just like I had to fall in love with me. The time of believing you are "un" anything is over, and you will begin choosing beliefs that build you up instead of tear you down—beliefs that align with who you truly are or at least desire to be.

Remember, your odyssey is a journey.

It has never been a race.

I would say some of my biggest pitfalls during this experience have been related to me trying to rush the process. We did not develop these core beliefs overnight and they will not be removed immediately. It will take work. It will also take time. This work and time aid in every journey or transformation, something I call The 4 A's: Awareness, Acknowledgement, Acceptance, and Action. These core beliefs can begin to overcome any self-doubt, limiting beliefs and fears.

Every day I wake and look at a woman who loves fully. I am super proud of this person I have grown into, but it does not mean I don't have days where I still fight the voice in my head, telling me I am not enough. Yet that is a battle I have learned to win because I now know I am indeed enough. Not only do I know I am enough, but I also have specific steps and tools in place to help me recognize just how whole I am!

To know something about yourself is beautiful. To practice what you know is the full experience, just like saying "to know better is to do better." Healing is not a destination; it is a journey—one that will take you to the valleys and peaks of your very existence.

My clients get an ear-full, all the time, about how I don't care about what they know. And that's not literal, but what we are after is embodiment—*the be-ing*—to put into practice what we know so we can reap the full rewards of our knowledge and be whole, be healed. Reaping these rewards will remind and show us just how amazing we are and can shift the lives we currently live into lives we desire, taking our wishes and turning them into destinations—places you can and will reach if you say yes to your journey.

chapter 3
Who Do You Love?

> *"We must reject not only the stereotypes that others hold of us, but also the stereotypes that we hold of ourselves."*
>
> —SHIRLEY CHISOLM

"Siri, play *Who Do You Love* by LL Cool J featuring Total." THERE IS A VERSE IN THIS SONG THAT says, "Who do you love? Are you for sure?" That is the question I am posing to you. Except I am more concerned with who do you love and how do you love them. Are you loving yourself with the same enthusiasm as you do others? Better yet, how about half the enthusiasm?

This is not the time or place to lie to yourself. If you took inventory of the way you love and care for yourself, could you say you're doing your best? And I want you to understand that doing your best does not mean daily sunshine and rainbows. No, doing your best is going to be unique to you and specific to your situation. Sometimes, doing my best looks like me doing nothing at all and just allowing myself to be. Other times, it's trips with friends to exotic places. It varies.

But what it does require is an in-depth relationship with *you*. Understanding what you need and giving yourself just that.

It requires grace. (Yes y'all, grace.) Because this relationship is not about getting it right; it's about learning what feeds you spiritually, mentally, and emotionally. And, that takes time.

For every broken heart and fallen tear, there is a rite of passage. My pain, my struggle, this beautiful journey of loving and finding myself is my rites of passage, and it is yours too. Rites of passages usually involve ritual activities and teachings designed to strip individuals of their original roles and prepare them for new ones. Would you believe me if I said everything you've been through up until this point was meant to prepare you for what's to come? I know this might be a little hard to believe, but it's true.

I know… I know…

You are probably thinking your life has prepared you for war, and there was a time I felt the same way about mine. But I now understand this isn't true. If it's not true for me, then it cannot be true for you either. This life will bring out of us what we need to rid ourselves of and to grow from. The moment you begin to see life is not happening to you but for you, things begin to change drastically.

You are no longer helpless.

You are no longer looking for someone to come and save you.

That guy who promised you the world and ran your credit up before leaving did you a favor. He pointed out to you that you were settling for less than you deserve, and from that place you can choose. There is always a choice. You can decide to look at your actions up to that point and take accountability, or you can stay in a cycle where you continue to attract the same man over and over.

During this rite of passage, you will either willingly relinquish the things that no longer serve you, or you will continue to suffer trying to hold on to them. I pray you choose your elevation instead of clinging in desperation to your continuous suffering. Allow your lessons, though they may be hard, to strip you of all the things that have held you back and leave you reborn—as a woman who is bruised but not broken, who is wise and soft, who can be firm and kind, who is living her life and not their lies. It's time for you to choose to shine!

As you are reading this, I hope you find it abundantly clear that the power and change you've craved for so long can only come from you. No one, and I mean no one outside of you, will ever be able to give you that feeling of safety.

Becoming Her is not about going to a new place but returning home to your truth. You are returning back to your true self, the self you were before you met and embraced the coldness of the world. What truth is that? That you innately shine without having to do anything! That it is your birth right to shine.

I get it. After years of being hurt, maybe even abused and told you were not good enough, you began to believe it. And each time you took someone else's "truth" as your own, you put another cloak over your light.

I am inviting you to not only take those cloaks off but to no longer allow anyone else to put another one on. You get to choose, at any point, when someone tries to give you their truth or opinion not to take it on as yours. Something I have gotten into the practice of saying is "that doesn't feel true for me," and it is at that point when I know whatever they spouted will not enter into my spirit. It isn't mine to carry.

On your journey, you will begin to discover things about yourself that you either never knew or never took the time to pay attention to. I don't want this to happen, unintentionally. I believe we can slip in and out of relationship with ourselves because we are not being intentional with ourselves. The purpose of *Becoming Her* is to learn how to practice being consciously aware of our intentions toward ourselves and allow ourselves to flourish endlessly. From my journey and time with therapists and coaches, I recognized there were four major areas I needed to develop daily: Self-awareness, Self-respect, Self-confidence, and Self-trust. These major areas, coupled with acknowledgment and acceptance, are the reason I am here today. And when I say here today, I mean alive and not just living—alive and enjoying every part of my life!

By learning and loving myself first, I have opened the doors to a happiness and a peace that was once foreign to me. From my personal experience I can vouch that, if practiced regularly, you will see positive effects throughout your life. Attending to your needs emotionally, physically, mentally and spiritually is one of the most important things you can do; it is vital to your overall health and well-being. Paying attention to yourself has a lasting impact on your personal reality and the reality you share with others. Creating daily routines that help to develop and express these practices and attributes will only help to strengthen and further encourage a deep-rooted love for yourself.

It is also important to understand that what you are about to read is a story of action. Something I taught myself and now teach other women is that courage is the secret ingredient to live a life fulfilled. And my recipe for courage is faith plus action. *That's right!*

Faith + Action = Courage

You may never feel truly ready, and your willingness may be fleeting, but you know what needs to be done. The relationship you are building with yourself will require you to go into the darkest parts of yourself—places and spaces of your heart and soul that you barricaded and barb wired off because of the pain caused to you. *We're going there.*

This is not something I recommend you do alone. Create a community, which can include your therapist and also exclude yo' mama 'nem. Understand what you need so you can surround yourself with who you need. Everything isn't for everybody and that is okay. Courageous women find strength in being supported and building their community—emphasis on their. To build your community, you must begin to understand who you are and where it is you are going. If you do not exercise this type of self-awareness, you will be surrounded by people and still feel alone.

I know it may feel like I am asking a lot by telling you to build a relationship with the darkest parts of yourself and inviting others in when I know you've fought hard to look away from them. However, I know from personal experience that I could have easily gone into a deeper hole and the depths of anger, depression and despair replacing the life budding inside after such huge losses. I could not have made it to where I am alone, so allow yourself to be supported in the most nourishing ways. On the other side of it awaits the abundance, grace and love you deserve that I now experience from the choices I made in the midst of my own storm. These new choices have elevated and allowed me to create the life of fulfillment I currently have and offer you.

Yes, it felt like an eternity for me to begin believing just how wonderfully made I am.

No, I don't want you to face it alone.

As a child, my mother often told me how precious I was—how valuable and worthy I was—but I had allowed my life circumstances and bad decisions to dictate who I allowed myself to be and to believe I was. Now, I can finally speak about my greatness without trying to shy away from or shrink it. I can speak about love and forgiveness from a place of knowing it intimately. This is the tale of the redeemed. *Becoming Her* is my story, and it is available to you—should you choose it.

Yes, I am a firm believer that everyone should know how amazing they are. But I don't only want you to know it; I want you to feel it. The sense of knowingness that comes with accepting who you are and allowing the light within you to shine—no matter what your past says about you—is a gift and so are you.

At some point in our lives, we have all deemed ourselves unworthy based on past actions and mistakes. Some of us get stuck there. Most of us don't even realize it. We let our shame, guilt, and fear take over the voice in our head, and we allow it to decide what we deserve.

Today you are going to take charge of that little voice. That voice that says, "Give up," "I can't do that," "I'm not qualified enough," and "I'm not pretty enough, in shape enough..." That voice that only pushes the not enoughness agenda. Today we are going to grab it by the reins and say, "No more!" We are putting that voice on reassignment, refocusing its attention on all the beautiful things you are, and invoking the spirit of abundance and denouncing the spirit of lack. Because you have that type of power.

If you allow it that voice will teach you how to uplift and encourage. It will begin to speak more light and love than doom and gloom. We are not here seeking perfection but instead acceptance—acceptance of who you are and what has brought you here, acceptance of the fact that you are deserving of love, despite what you've been through. You were created with, in, and on purpose. This type of acceptance cultivates a space for progression, and that is the goal.

Life may have seemed unfair and felt like you could catch a cold before you ever caught a break, and it is that mindset that we are throwing away. Nothing is happening to you; it is always happening for you. No matter how many times you feel that you have struck out, your time is and will always be right now. It is my hope that *Becoming Her* helps you to build up those parts of you that you deemed un…

Unforgivable.

Unlovable.

Unseen.

Unheard.

Something I want to make astoundingly clear is that the very things about yourself that you work so hard to hide are the exact things that will connect you to your tribe. The people who are around you whom you may feel are using you or aren't really your friends, you've attracted them. They are friends with the persona you choose to put on every day. Is it possible that people may not be able to connect with you deeply because you haven't been willing to connect with yourself deeply, causing a disconnection in all areas of your life? If all your relationships feel shallow, dip your toe in your own pool and see how far it goes.

I am not trying to make you feel bad; it's just the opposite. I want you to recognize a powerful tool you have readily available at your disposal: The ability to impact. Your very environment is a direct reflection of you. If you want more depth in your external relationships, it's going to start with the relationship you have going on internally. If you can recognize that you have an impact on how your life is going, then you will begin to understand the power you have to change it.

Most of our lives we spend feeling like we are in it alone—in our pain alone, struggling alone, that no one truly understands. But, that's a lie. It is a lie that has been ingrained and used to help keep you protected. And that lie is costing you all the connections, love, laughter, and support you desire. I'm not saying it won't be scary, but it doesn't have to be hard and lonely. Begin releasing the parts of you that are holding you back. Open yourself up to new opportunities and watch the sunflower bloom out of the darkness. It will find the light it needs, and so will you.

The question is do you truly believe you deserve more? Are you willing to be open to it? If you don't believe you are worth it or are unsure right now, keep reading. Allow yourself to believe you are more than your mistakes and deserving of the things that will elevate your entire life.

chapter 4
Breaking up with Grace

"I'm no longer accepting the things I cannot change... I'm changing the things I cannot accept."

—ANGELA DAVIS

GRACE IS DEFINED AS THE FREE and <u>unmerited</u> favor of God, as <u>manifested</u> in the salvation of <u>sinners</u> and the bestowal of blessings, per Oxford Languages. My mother always quotes me the Serenity Prayer, especially when I am going through a tough time. If you are unfamiliar with this prayer it goes like this: "God, grant me the serenity to accept the things I cannot change, courage to change the things I can, and wisdom to know the difference."

This prayer is one of the many seeds of courage planted within me as a child. But the grace my mother told me about, and the one I had developed, was very different. What grace became for me over time, starting at an early age, was an underlying belief that I could hold the problems and mistakes of others; I had the power to hold it and fix it for them. I remember my oldest brother facing some really serious charges, and all I wanted was for God to hear me. *God, please don't take my brother.* I prayed, knowing I could extend my grace.

By extending grace, it meant nothing "bad" would happen. My concept of good and bad was very linear, living by the ethos of avoiding pain by any means necessary. And when my brother was sentenced to 15 years in prison, there was a little part of me that felt I had failed. As the years went on, and I kept trying to extend my own grace—this ultimate protection—I kept being disappointed, internalizing each letdown as if it were my responsibility and fault. I was incapable of helping, and God obviously could not hear me.

This concept nibbled away at my confidence and over the years aided in my belief that I was not enough, that I was not capable. It reverberated through me that I should get used to the bad because that is all I deserved.

I remember wishing to live the lives of my white friends because their lives seemed less complicated, almost effortless. As an adult, I now know that was untrue and, quite frankly, I wouldn't change one part of my story. (But we will get to that later.) Wielding my convoluted concept of grace to be extended to my father, mother, brothers, and sister, this extension was also gifted to my husband and children because I love them and did not want anything "bad" to ever happen to them either. And when the "bad" did happen, my belief in grace (myself) diminished.

What the heck was wrong with my grace?

When was it going to kick in and stop every single bad thing from happening to me and those I love?

Writing this out makes me laugh, but I really believed this y'all. I thought I was capable of shielding everyone I love from anything "bad" happening to them. And the hit to my self-confidence when things didn't work out was real, no matter how unreasonable my request. At this point, I wanted to say, "Fuck Grace and the set she rep."

Nah, but seriously, I was over her. And her was me. I was not saying "fuck grace" every time I was let down. I was saying, "fuck Laniece."

"Fuck, Laniece. Why can't you protect everything and everyone you love?" If I continued down this path, the only one who would continue to suffer was me.

Suffering can become quite addictive. And I was no exception to how luring and comfortable the "woe is me" life is. Yeah, I was habitually thinking about how terrible my life was and the decisions I did or didn't make. How "if this was different," my life would be better, or "if he didn't…" or "if she did…"

Every single thing was outside of my control, forever victim. Nah, I can't go out like that.

After we lost the twins, I slowly came to the realization that victim wasn't a title I was comfortable carrying anymore. So, I decided to call it quits. Before that, "I am not a quitter" was something I had become accustomed to saying. So many people in my life had been judged as being incomplete—*by* me. I would not be one of them.

Listen, I don't believe quitting—in and of itself—is a bad trait. However, for many years, I was so misguided. This caused me to hold onto relationships that only reinforced my low self-esteem. I was Pickmesha or Pick-Me-Anna, searching for something (or someone) to see the value in me that I could not recognize in myself. Reflecting on this now fills me with a sense of sadness and joy because I know how empty I felt. And to now have an intimate relationship with forgiveness is liberating. To know what it feels like to give myself *exactly* what I so badly craved, mhmmm grateful. So now that you know I am not a quitter, let's continue.

I decided to approach grace a bit differently. I was not giving up on this relationship with grace, neither was I giving up on the new relationship with myself and how grace now applied—not without a fight. There were two versions of me at play here: The Laniece, who used grace like "Fix a Flat," and the budding version that understood I had no idea what grace was or how to use it. To be honest, the latter was scary because it was the unknown. I was comfortable in my not-enoughness. It was familiar. Some days, it was killing me; other days were good.

My internal dialogue often fought for my limitations because life wasn't *that* bad. This was a mental and emotional tug of war because my old ways of being had endured so much pain under the falsehood of grace. I was bonded to my misunderstanding of it. *What if this is as good as it gets?* All the doubt began to rise, but my inner voice was persistent like, "Girl, we ain't staying here. I don't care what's over on the other side. We're about to go see."

Those steps brought me to the reality that I could redefine the meaning of grace in my life. Knowing the way I conceptualized and applied it before was more of wishful thinking instead of acceptance and acknowledgment of what is. I wanted to be distant from the pain and reality and still have a major impact. And the truth is, that's just not possible. If someone is bleeding out, you can't stand on the sidelines and wish for them to live. You must get down and apply direct pressure. And that means getting close to the wounds and all the messiness of the blood, but the sooner you do, the better chance that person has to live. Are you ready to apply direct pressure to your open wounds? This is the work of healing and changing underlying beliefs: Having a willingness to objectively look at ourselves, regardless of the discomfort it may cause.

chapter 5
Renewing Grace

"Your devotion to others was it just your excuse from forging your own path?"

—CAPTAIN ONE PIECE

DEVELOPING A NEW BELIEF TAKES TIME and practice. Before I could extend anything to anyone else, I first needed to understand what it meant to and for me. My childhood belief turned into my adult avoidance. It was the excuses I used to keep myself small and inadequate. While we are talking about grace, this is true in every aspect of life, especially love. It is our beliefs that create our reality. I had to understand what grace was to me, for me, and by me before I started trying to extend it all willy-nilly. This was not an easy process because, by this point, I had over twenty plus years of not understanding or applying grace to me. It was a luxury I could not afford because I subconsciously created the belief that I was not worthy of it. Therefore, whatever I had should be given away to those I thought deserved it. *Wrong!*

I slowly learned that the first person I am responsible for giving grace to for the rest of my life is me. Grace is not this magic conduit that protects us and everything we love from hardship. It is forgiveness and the opportunity to say, "What is here for me?" Grace is giving yourself time to learn the lesson that came with the "bad." It's the opportunity to understand that nothing is ever truly bad but is a test for your testament—proof that everything you endured was not for naught, that you have the opportunity to come out on the other side wiser than before. And this all boils down to choice.

The moment I began to choose what grace meant to me and started applying it to my life so much changed. I looked at myself in the mirror and began seeing a woman staring back at me with a peace about her—a peace that I can only imagine I felt at birth and as a young child. It was my opportunity to allow myself to be reborn, free of all the pain I once carried as a badge of honor. I looked at a woman who was lighter, who was beautiful. Not because of what I looked like, but because of what I felt like. I no longer felt underserving; I no longer felt unseen or unheard. I finally took the time to see me, to hear me, and to love me.

With my newfound belief and practice of grace, I released myself from the shame and guilt that came with carrying the load of other's burdens. I began to understand that my only concern when extending my grace to others was through the form of forgiveness. My grace evolved into looking past a person's transgressions and seeing them for the hurt soul in need. The way I viewed the entire world shifted. Because of that, I practiced grace everywhere (from traffic to the supermarket), understanding there are people who feel similar to how I once felt: Underserving, unseen, and unheard. And while I would never carry their shame or guilt, I can give the best gift possible: Grace.

Grace can come by way of a smile and patience. It can be a random compliment to remind a person that you see them. Grace for my children is recognizing that they made a mistake but not loving them any differently because of it. That was a huge one for me. Learning not to be the constant reminder of mistakes for the people I love was hard.

I can remember being that person who would rummage through my memory bank of "how you did me wrong" or "that time when you let me down" to remind people that they were not worthy. That may not have been what I said, but it's definitely what I meant. And ughhhh, it makes me so sad sometimes because I cannot take that back, and that is where grace comes in. I will never be able to take any of it back. However, I can choose to live in the newness of my now understanding of grace and give myself a break.

There's a saying that "hurt people, hurt people." Let's personalize it. Hurt mothers, hurt their daughters. Hurt wives, hurt their husbands. Hurt fathers, hurt their sons. Hurt husbands, hurt their wives. It can go on and on and on. Yet we are not just hurting random people; we are hurting the very ones we say we love so much. And to what end? This can become a vicious cycle, one that will prove your unconscious belief that you are not worthy.

When you push everyone away, and you're left with your self-loathing thoughts, then will you feel vindicated? Will you win? Trust me, it won't be in a way you truly desire. You will feel disconnected, isolated, and guilty. So today, since you were kind enough to stick your nose into this book, I am extending grace to you too. *Not the first version, of course.*

This is your reminder that you are perfectly placed in your story right now and have the most powerful tool to change anything you desire: Choice. You can choose to believe the thoughts that lead to unworthiness, or you can choose grace. Feel free to adopt my version or to create your own. Just make sure it's one that leaves you feeling full, not empty.

We are not perfect beings. I still get irritated when my kids are on 1000%, and my husband is asking me what's for dinner.

"Dinner… I'm not even hungry."

That might not be my exact response, but I know I can give a "tude" that lets him know I am on edge. Why? Because I am a growing being, and each day my patience gets better and better. And my family are the ones who allow me to practice working on it. It's the work I choose for my life.

Understanding that you don't have to be a bystander in how your life plays out will be beyond important. Choice is power. You have choices, which means at birth you were powerful.

Say it with me, "I am powerful!"

And I'm not talking about some weak affirmation. I want you to go in front of the mirror and see that amazing reflection staring back at you, screaming at the top of your lungs, "I AM POWERFUL."

For far too long, we let our environment dictate who we can be and how we can be it. When we lack self-awareness, giving true attention and intention to the decisions that shape our lives can feel hard. Instead, we become sitting freaking ducks for anyone to misuse and take advantage of. Even worse, we accept less because we have tricked ourselves into believing this is what we deserve. And to that, I say, *"Heck no!"*

Becoming Her is not a book that will ask you to shift the blame to everyone who has mistreated you. Nope, exactly the opposite. Go to the mirror right now and say "sorry." Apologize to the person who stands before you. Apologize for accepting anything less than what you deserve or desire.

Shame and guilt from things that happened to us as children, as teenagers, as young adults, and even up until today have kept us small. We developed beliefs of being less than and unworthy because of neglect and abuse. Some of us dimmed our lights and others turned them off completely. I am here to tell you that is not the answer. The answer is, however, your own bestowal of grace—your choice to forgive yourself for how you let the world treat you and how you allowed that mistreatment to define who you would become.

Before you start the work below, I want you to know this is an invitation. Every single idea or tool I provide is an invitation. It is not law. I am not challenging you to love yourself more. I am inviting you into a new way of being, thinking, living, and loving. And now that you've been invited, you get to choose what you will do with the invitation.

INVITATION:

You Get What You Believe You Deserve

GRACE MAY NOT HAVE BEEN at the center of your limiting beliefs, but they are all centered around something. And if you're willing, I'd like to give you a gentle hand in finding what those resonating centers are. This is not a one-and-done process. You can continue this practice until your soul says move on. But first, you must prioritize the time to focus on yourself. This may feel selfish, depending on your current circumstances. And if it does feel selfish to carve out time for you, then this is not a request; it is a demand. I am joking, but only kinda sorta. The time for you is now.

I want you to get into a quiet space. This is a place where you can be alone with yourself and your thoughts. Give yourself thirty minutes to an hour. Put it on your schedule… Make you a priority. I want you to think about your life and the underlying belief that may be ruling your reality. I will provide a list of examples below. Remember, this is not something you need to get right the first time. This is an exploration. It can take time to get to the root. But first, you must begin to look. Along the way, discoveries will happen. You will open, and the weight will begin to lift.

EXAMPLES OF LIMITING CORE BELIEFS:
- I don't deserve to be loved or treated well.
- My achievements are not as significant as others'.
- I'm not attractive enough to be in a relationship.

- I don't have the skills to be successful.
- People will leave me if they see the real me.
- I can't be happy until I meet certain standards.

If these resonate with you, feel free to use them. However, if they don't, I need you to be honest with yourself, as much as possible, until you find something true as to who and where you are. Once you have something, write it out (remember to do this as many times as you need).

ANSWER THE FOLLOWING QUESTIONS:
1. Why do you think this is true?
2. What experiences have led you to this conclusion?
3. How does this belief influence your actions or decisions?
4. What do you think is the opposite of this belief, and why do you reject it?
5. What would it take for you to change your mind about this?
6. Who or what influences your beliefs on this topic?

Write your answers. Every time you think of where you did not choose you because of this belief, know the silent cost was your very being. This is where the self-betrayal ends and uncovering your true essence begins. Write them out, and don't get shy now. This is not the time to worry about grammar or writing neatly. I need you to pour as freely as you possibly can. Empty yourself out!

Hear me… I get it. You may have never said any of these things out loud, and you've possibly kept them hidden from yourself and everyone else. But consider how that has served you, so far, then continue.

After writing your answers walk away. Grab a glass of water because this can be intense. Once you're hydrated, return to that notebook and read what you wrote aloud. There is a healing and a connection that happens when taking pen to paper you should welcome. Allow yourself to feel that wave of emotion that is flooding your body as you read your own handwriting and hear your own voice. Is it sadness, anger, or grief? It may be a mixture of all three. Whatever it is that comes up *for you*, you get to feel it. You will no longer deny yourself the right to process what feels real in your body. Live and grow through it.

Now, I want you to take a moment, close your eyes, and ask yourself who would you be without this belief. I don't want you to write it out; I want you to envision who you would be if you didn't believe that everything had to be a struggle or if you believed you were **always** capable and deserving. Allow yourself to get lost in your amazingness. Is this version of you laughing and smiling? How does she feel? Is she lighter? Who is she?

I want to let you in on a little surprise... She is already here. This version of you exists and is waiting for you to make the choices that allow her to flourish. Now walk to that bathroom mirror, get your handy-dandy dry-erase marker, and write I AM HER!

Let this simple yet powerful affirmation be a reminder to the woman you are becoming, the one who no longer allows those limiting beliefs to dictate her worthiness. The woman you were created to be. This is the beginning of a new belief—your new belief that you are worthy... Worthy of your own love and forgiveness. This is not a magic exercise. You will not miraculously be free of your own thoughts and guilt. This is, however, an opening. It is an introduction to a new belief, a new practice, a new you. So, when those thoughts do arise, you can remind yourself that you deserve grace.

chapter 6
Creating the Space

"We cannot solve our problems with the same thinking we used when we created them."

—ALBERT EINSTEIN

NOW THAT YOU UNDERSTAND (and maybe you have even adopted some of what I believe grace to be), let me introduce you to something I discovered on my own but found out to be ancient wisdom: Since the beginning of time, space has been a necessity for growth. I believe we were meant to experience all parts of this life. I also believe that our beautiful self-portraits are being painted with the bright red of our pain and the clearest yellow of our joy. And every experience is needed to create the masterpiece that is you. And I believe, sometimes, we forget about our access to unlimited hues and colors and begin moving through life stuck using just one.

Throughout this book, you will see me referring to an emptiness within myself that felt insatiable. My relationship with "emptiness" had to grow through some changes as well. I had to learn to become intentional with what I emptied. You see, before developing this relationship with myself, I held onto every memory of mistreatment and missed opportunity, so much so that I had a playlist on my phone that could take me right back to the exact feelings so that I could relive them over and over. I remember, one time specifically, my husband asking me, "Do you want to stay sad?" as I started on one of my self-loathing binges, blasting my "life sucks and it's hard to be me" music after receiving some bad news.

Immediately, I was offended because I was **triggered.** The nerve of him telling me the truth, but my ego was too loud to hear him. I clung to the belief that I was always misunderstood and responded in sarcasm—my go-to—because I could not admit that I was addicted to my pain, continuously allowing the words from those songs to reaffirm the not-enoughness that weighed heavily on my shoulders. It wasn't until the past five years that I realized I was constantly on the hunt for something or someone to love the unlovable parts of me that I never actually allowed them to see.

Listen, you cannot teach someone how to love you in your entirety when you do not know or love yourself in your entirety. Think of it as giving street-by-street directions to a place you've never been from memory to a person who's never been there, nor do they know it even exists—a classic case of "the blind leading the blind." If you can relate to this, then you, my friend, have been a surface dweller—only allowing yourself to show what you deem acceptable. And the requirements for this acceptance were heavily shaped on societal views and the not-enoughness you've tried to bury behind accomplishments and material possessions. If this isn't you, then good. It is still good for you to have an understanding that there are people in your life who operate from this space: Empty.

I am serious. If that is you, I want you to dwell in the emptiness you've created.

Okay, maybe some clarification is needed here. I am not talking about the emptiness that is created out of not-enoughness and unfulfillment. I am talking about intentional emptying, decluttering, and the purifying of your entire being. I want you to feel so light that you open yourself to infinite possibilities. This is what creating intentional space feels like. There is a difference; trust me.

There is the type of emptiness that eats away at you and another kind that promotes life and growth. One can happen unconsciously and is often the remnants of past and present trauma, while the other is an intentional form of release around the very experiences that promoted your self-deprecation. From this day forward, you have been exposed to the choice. You get to choose between walking around feeding your own personal black hole or removing the debris of past hurt and trauma. It's up to you.

As a society, we've grown accustomed to hoarding things mentally, physically, emotionally, and spiritually. I was no exception to this off-brand version of self-inflicted torture. And what I am inviting you into is the emptying—emptying the stuff that keeps you bound, the stuff that you believe is "as good as it gets."

Becoming Her is not the book that is going to tell you to settle. I am not the person who will encourage you to embrace mediocrity when I genuinely believe you deserve extraordinary.

Many of us have been accepting people, positions, roles, and things into our lives "as is." Our standards have been low and maybe even nonexistent. We start to get excited about the bare minimum efforts of others and to constant smaller wins ourselves. I've been there, and I promise you there is more. Not only is there more, but it is your birthright to have it. You must require more to receive it. The question is, do you believe me? Even if you're skeptical, are you willing to come and find out what's over here? It is time for you to create the space for your evolution, and I welcome you to do it.

A quote by Dr. Jacob Moreno, one of the pioneers of psychotherapy, says, "The body remembers what the mind forgets." The thoughts and behaviors you have created live not only in your mind but are also stored in your body. You may have been able to push some traumatic experiences into the depths of your mind, but your body's response to that trauma is what creates the triggers. Have you ever wondered why something so simple could make you so mad? Likely because, there is something bigger lying beneath that anger. Whatever we address in the mind, we will also address in the body.

Space is needed to plant new seeds of abundance and prosperity. But first, you must root out the beliefs of lack and limitation—any belief that makes you feel you are underserving, unseen, unheard, or unlovable. This next exercise has allowed me to create space within my body and the women I have supported over the years. I encourage you not to rush the work. If you get to this part and can't do it now, don't. It is not my intention that you "squeeze in" your healing. That would further defeat the purpose of what we are doing. Also notice any excuses that may come up around making space for you; that voice is the opposition you will continuously face until it becomes natural to make yourself a priority.

INVITATION:
Emptying

CREATING SPACE INTERNALLY and externally is going to be important as you continue along your journey.

Reflective Journaling Prompts

IDENTIFYING CLUTTER:
What areas of your life feel cluttered or overwhelming right now?

Reflect on physical spaces, relationships, work, and internal thoughts. List them out in your journal.

ASSESSING IMPACT:
How does this clutter affect your mental and physical well-being?

Write about specific instances where you felt stressed, anxious, or drained due to lack of space.

DEFINING SPACE:
What does creating space mean to you?

Describe what a more spacious, balanced life looks and feels like.

PRIORITIZING AREAS:
Which area of your life needs the most immediate attention for creating space?

Rank the areas you've identified and focus on the top one or two.

SETTING INTENTIONS:
What steps can you take to create more space in your body and life?

Write down realistic, actionable steps for both physical and mental decluttering.

VISUALIZING OUTCOMES:
Visualize and describe how your life will improve once you've created more space.

Reflect on the positive changes you expect to see and feel.

Practice this as often as your life allows, especially when you feel overwhelmed. The aim is that this becomes so ingrained in some way, shape, or form that you find yourself being less and less overwhelmed.

chapter 7
The Coupling

"Blindly seeking to destroy what we fear also destroys the opportunity that we have to grow from it."

—CRAIG D. LOUNSBROUGH

NOW THAT YOU UNDERSTAND THE importance of your relationship with space and grace, let's combine them. For me, there is no better way toward growth.

Space or grace can exist without the other; however, it is a painful path. Why? Because, if you give yourself space to try something new and you fail and lack grace, it will be difficult for you to overcome that failure and try again. It will be difficult to see the blessing in that failure and take from it what was meant to be taken. Grace allows you to feel the pain of that failure and the wisdom to look at what is there for you to learn.

Yes, I said feel the pain. Pain can grow into a beautiful experience. Don't believe me? Let me give you a personal example. Some years after losing the twins and getting into coaching, I created a workshop called Becoming Her. When I created it, I was fully connected to the grief of losing my babies and the person I was before them. I tapped into the pain of what I wished I had before them and what I had to build after them, and it gave birth to this incredibly transformative workshop that I now take all over the world to women who need it. The only word to describe that is *beautiful*. Pain can be the catalyst for you to begin creating from a space of alignment. It is a reminder that we are here and that we have loved or desired something, the absence of which has left a lasting impact. Once the impact is made, it is your choice how you choose to move forward.

If you allow it, pain can be an indicator of passion. I always had a passion for serving, but the twins showed me my path—a path I would have never had the courage to find if not for them. It takes courage to allow your pain to be transmuted into your passion because that is not the societal norm. We often use our pain to fuel the reasons why we can't. The first sign of adversity and struggle, most people tend to give up. To have a passion that you actively seek out is courageous. So, in my book—both literally and figuratively—you are already amongst the few who dare to see what's beyond complacency, which makes you extraordinary.

Both space and grace require something to enact their limitless powers: Awareness. You must know yourself well enough to be able to call upon the powers of space and grace. The invitations you have been given so far will begin to build that relationship.

Do you know what happens when you weaponize your pain and begin using it as an identity to keep you safe? You become hardened. You may feel protected for a time, but eventually that protection becomes a block. As a coach, I understand from my own personal experience that we often lean towards pain and punishment instead of rest and relaxation. We have turned rest into this revolutionary concept when, in fact, it is a fundamental requirement. It is only revolutionary because we've denied ourselves it for so long. In turn, we opt to agonize over our mistakes and withhold our own release of said mistakes, which blocks us from experiencing joy, happiness, love, and peace—the ultimate fulfillment.

For me, understanding my relationship with willful suffering was a game-changer. It took me to a new level of self-awareness. To sit back now and think, *I chose suffering*. You're probably thinking, Laniece, no one chooses to suffer. But, I have experienced too much to know differently. Here's a quick way to see if you are choosing to willingly suffer. Reflect on a current challenge you're facing. If there is an action you can take to improve the situation but you're choosing not to, ask yourself why. This is a form of willful suffering. Reflecting on everything, I came to the realization that I had built a cozy home in my misery, which still amazes me. *Like, wow.* But sometimes, we are so deeply involved that we just can't see it. I could not accept what I could not see. My lack of self-awareness hindered my ability to see and accept my part in my circumstances, which ultimately kept me from standing in my power.

There is so much power in self-awareness. Actively practicing this will help you to understand and evaluate your daily choices. Just like I can set up a house in misery and suffering, I can build a home in abundance and joy. It's time for you to open your mind, heart, and soul and take inventory. Where are your choices leading you astray and out of alignment? Allow yourself to be aware of the part you play and recognize where you are standing in your own way. Once you start doing this, you will redirect your superpower. You will begin to make aligned decisions to the woman you are becoming—*Her*.

Grace is coupled with space because it is an extension of mercy. Not to bore you with definitions, but again I'll quote Oxford Languages. "Mercy is defined as compassion or forgiveness shown toward someone whom it is within one's power to punish or harm." No one can punish you, like you can punish you. And for many women, we allow ourselves to become our own worst enemy. This too is a choice. One you can make consciously or unconsciously.

I am urging you to move into the conscious realm of choice. While you are discovering who you are and how to truly love yourself, you will need to extend yourself some mercy—forgiveness. Forgiveness is the key to releasing any part of yourself from the self-imposed purgatory created by your limited beliefs.

chapter 8
Moving Pots (Doing the Necessary Work)

"What you seek is seeking you. Look within."

—RUMI

I mentioned earlier that I "moved pots and kept my soil." Remember that? (Page 29)

WELL, WE ALL KNOW THAT IF YOU plant a seed in a small container, it will be limited in its growth. But if you take that same seed and plant it in a larger container, it will begin to flourish. But there's so much more to creating space for a plant to flourish. There's the soil, the pot, the seeds, water and potential direct sunlight. So much intention and attention must go into that plant for it to thrive, and the same is true for you.

For far too long I had planted myself in beliefs that had me believing I was less than. And every single day, I tried to prove myself wrong and wound up with accomplishment after accomplishment being fed into my personal black hole. Eventually, I had to slow down and learn about my planting process. You see, I could go get a new pot and plant new seeds and completely ignore the evidence of that other pot. Kind of like ef them seeds and their bad harvest. And that's exactly what I did, but to myself, completely turning a blind eye to what I did or did not create and started anew. But if I continued doing that would I know anything about what actually needed to be planted, or how to tend to it? Or would I just be bringing my current skill level to a new pot and messing it up all over again?

For a while, I was the latter—moving from pot to pot with the same level of knowledge and understanding, hoping this time would be different. Hoping, with one eye open, that this time I would bear the fruit I had always longed for, just to end up with the same bitter berries from the last pot.

This can become a vicious cycle. Because the pots represent relationships, jobs, finances, etc. It literally touches everything. After multiple failed attempts, I realized it wasn't just my seeds but my soil. This revelation occurred after significant pain and loss, but the evidence was always there. I was just too close (and too closed-off) to it.

My hope is that it won't take you a considerable loss to bring awareness to you. The realization that my foundation was always the same, no matter what seeds I planted, changed my life. My soil reeked of not-enoughness—the belief that no matter what I did, I'd always be lacking, a step behind, undeserving. The guilt and shame transferred from one beautiful pot to another. I had to understand my soil, my foundation, in which I had been planted—the beliefs I carried unconsciously and consciously. This took time and it was painful.

I hold the belief that before we can truly break through anything, we must first accept it in ourselves, by ourselves. No one pointing out that your pot stinks and is full of holes is going to make you truly change. You may patch a hole here and there, but patching is only good enough to mask the faulty foundation. It's the equivalence of putting a Band-Aid over a gunshot wound. No, accepting and being willing to dig up your own dirt takes intentionality. It is an inside job; you must care that it stinks. You have to open yourself up to even recognize there's a smell to begin with. So, accepting that stench and everything that comes with it is critical. Accepting lays the groundwork for you to begin replanting, regrowing, and rebuilding. It is the complete opposite of patchwork. Groundwork is mental, emotional, physical, and spiritual. Patchwork is not. It is only physical. Patchwork is aesthetically pleasing. Groundwork is aesthetically repelling.

Long story short, acceptance means you must move out of your denial. This translates to acknowledging that you played a major part in your life's current stinky, holy pot.

We go through life living on accident, at least I know I did. I so badly wanted things to just "work out," but I didn't want to do the work. And I was so hard-working.

You're probably like, "Laniece, make that make sense."

Well, I worked harder for other people's dreams and convictions than my own. I could see greatness in others (and even foster hope and promote courage for them), but I did not know how to do it for myself. I did not know my process, and because I was afraid to take the hard looks at me, I focused my attention outwardly. *Am I the only one?*

When you believe you're a lost cause, it feels good to help someone else see how beautiful and gifted they are. Because, you are too broken to be either. There's too much to unpack…too much work to do. So, you focus on them.

My question is, if you don't ever see and understand why it is you move the way you move, where are you leading yourself? Even better question: If you're a parent, where are you leading your children?

At some point in your life, you choose to keep the blinders on. You accept that life is as it is and make no attempt to figure anymore of it out, believing it's easier to pretend things don't exist around you—like, chaos. But pain has a funny way of seeping through the cracks. It manifests in ways that stifle your ability to receive or give love in its fullness, manifesting into your short tempers and mental checkouts. And who benefits from this…suffering that you do? You continuously feed it by not acknowledging it exists.

Before you can move to a new pot, tend to your soil. Many of us have lived in these small containers for so long that our comfortability has also led to us feeling trapped and maxed out. And it is your God-given right to move.

But what are you bringing into your new home? Taking to your next level?

Some of us have been doing the work on ourselves, and maybe you're stuck in a place that can no longer support the person you are meant to become. If that is the case, I want you to consciously move into bigger spaces, discovering and realizing who it is you are becoming. By the end of this book, I want you to own that space if you currently do not.

Be unapologetic!

Become Her.

It is your personal playground to experience and design life as you see fit. You have more control over your life and journey than you have been practicing, and it's time for you to start acting like it.

chapter 9

Something on the Inside, Working on the Outside (Power of Joy)

> *"To challenge the status quo and find true joy, we must redefine our own narratives and reject the limitations imposed by others."*
>
> —KIMBERLÉ CRENSHAW

YOUR JOURNEY GETS TO BE EXACTLY what you make it. One of the biggest compliments I get from the women I have worked with is that I have a way of bringing joy into the heavy parts of healing. That was something I had innately but learned how to wield during my most difficult tests. It took practice, and fortunately, I had enough to happen in my life to learn how to cultivate my joy from within. And I did not use it as a Band-Aid or for escapism. I learned to be very present with all I was feeling while still allowing joy to weave in and out and all around my circumstances. They say practice makes perfect, so be careful what you practice.

What are you currently practicing?

Healing may feel hard and heavy, but joy is always readily available to you. You just need to figure out how to plug back into your source. And that is what I am here for.

Laughter is medicine. When we can learn to laugh at ourselves more, we are on the precipice of true healing.

Everything is about you, but mostly only to you. We are living in a society full of projections, where people are too consumed in themselves but not in a healthy, reflective way. Instead, they are consumed by their own insecurities and trauma. They then walk around, knowingly and unknowingly, spilling them onto other people—if not regurgitating them altogether. The projections you may face daily are from people still learning to navigate this life. This isn't a shot at them because they are us, and we are them. We are all going or growing through something. That is why we all deserve grace. I don't care how old one is; being stuck or choosing to grow has no time limit.

Let's be honest. We all take ourselves way too seriously. Every criticism or constructive feedback I received previously felt like a personal attack. I always felt the need to over-explain and make my point known with a face that let you know I wasn't the one. I was unable to receive assessments or evaluation in a way that could serve me. Instead, I responded to it as a threat. Until one day, I realized that my responses were a way to protect myself as I walked the streets of my childhood neighborhood or faced bullies at school. It was fine-tuned, and my comebacks were sharp, but I wasn't 10,15 or even 20 anymore.

Throughout my adult life, I found myself continuing a pattern of behavior that had its roots in my childhood experiences. It became evident that this behavior was hindering my personal growth. No matter where I moved or what the environment was, regardless of the good intentions behind the feedback I received, I never let my guard down. Even though I was in a physically safe environment, my body's response and nervous system remained on high alert, ready to protect me from anyone who might pose a threat. And guess what? Attached to this need to protect myself was a fear of failure. Yup, it can be layered. It often is. I once perceived their feedback as I had failed or let them down. The feedback was proof that I couldn't do it. The work that had to be done, y'all... The backsliding that inevitably happened... Your personal odyssey is granting you the ability to craft a new story and, as you progress, you will uncover parts of yourself that were previously inaccessible.

We get so caught up in how we are perceived that, along the way, we stop having fun with ourselves. Tell me how many times you think you fell as an infant until you figured out how to walk. You don't even remember; you just know you did it. That same resiliency exists inside of you now. It is not something you need to learn; it's something you need to allow—giving yourself the grace to be able to experience life in all its beauty and the wonders it has to offer... Falling and failing and giving it a go again because you know if you continue to take the lessons and apply them success is inevitable! The more time I spend learning from my mistakes and setbacks instead of trying to hide them from the world, the more I am in my truth and am able to grow—continuously learning to live from a place of knowing I don't have anything to prove to anyone but me.

In our fast-paced society, it's important for us to constantly remind ourselves that each person's life progresses at its own unique pace. With the pervasive influence of social media, it's easy for the lines between reality and artificial expectations to become blurred. The pressure to keep up with the curated lives and achievements of others can create a false sense of urgency in our own journeys. This can lead to unnecessary stress and a distorted perception of our personal timelines. Don't let them rush you. Your journey will have valleys and peaks, just like anyone else's, and your perspective can make something beautiful out of both settings.

As you embrace the journey of unlearning old habits and conditioning, it's important to give yourself the space and grace to embrace new experiences and learning opportunities. Remember that you are stepping into a new and exciting chapter of your life, and it has the potential to be the most fulfilling and rewarding one yet, as long as you open yourself up to it.

INVITATION:
Letting Joy Out

Finding joy in life can be a deeply enriching experience. Joy originates from within and can be cultivated by engaging in activities that bring nourishment to your soul. If you're struggling to find joy, it's important to take the time to nurture it on a daily basis.

Here are some ideas to help you begin this nurturing process:

1. Finding Joy in the Present:
One of the easiest ways to tap into joy is waking up with gratitude for being alive. I know there is a lot going on in your life and in this world, and today is another day to create something different. Bring mindful moments into your daily routine by setting aside a few minutes each day to sit quietly and to concentrate on your

breathing. Take the time to observe the sensations in your body, such as the rise and fall of your chest, the feeling of air passing through your nostrils, and the gentle expansion and contraction of your abdomen. Embrace the present moment with gratitude, acknowledging the simple beauty of being alive and the opportunity to experience the world around you.

2. Dance Break:
I LOVE TO DANCE. It is the quickest way for me to shift my mood and to change my perspective. Turn on your favorite music, close your eyes, and let the soothing melodies take over your senses. With each beat, let your body sway and move as if you were the only one in the room. Feel the music pulsing through your veins, igniting a sense of joy that radiates from within. Allow yourself to be completely immersed in the moment, embracing the freedom and euphoria that comes with dancing without inhibition. When it is all said and done, give words to describe how you feel in your body. Are you tingling all over, feeling light or warm?

3. Random Acts of Kindness:
Performing a random act of kindness for someone else can have a significant impact. It could be as simple as paying for someone's coffee at the cafe, surprising a friend with a small gift, giving a heartfelt compliment to a stranger, or writing a thank-you note to someone who has made a positive impact on your life. Kindness is one of the biggest gateways to joy, and the ripple effect of a single act of kindness can be immeasurable. It feels incredibly rewarding to help others feel good and to spread positivity in the world.

4. Nature Walk:
As you take a leisurely stroll in nature, take the time to truly immerse yourself in the stunning beauty that surrounds you. Take notice of the vibrant array of colors, from the rich greens of the foliage to the vivid hues of the flowers. Listen closely to the melodic symphony of bird songs, rustling leaves, and babbling brooks. Breathe in deeply and savor the earthy scents of the forest, the fresh aroma of the flowers, and the sweet fragrance of the air. As you

do so, allow yourself to forge a deep connection with the natural world, feeling the tranquility and joy it brings to your heart and soul.

5. Creative Expression

Take some time to engage in a creative activity that brings you joy and fulfillment. You could immerse yourself in painting, drawing, writing, or playing music. Allow yourself to let go of any self-judgment and instead focus on the pure joy of the creative process. Embrace the freedom to express yourself and to explore your imagination without any limitations. Let the act of creation be a source of relaxation and inspiration, allowing you to fully immerse yourself in the present moment.

chapter 10
Unforeseeable

*"A wise woman wishes to be no one's enemy;
a wise woman refuses to be anyone's victim."*

—MAYA ANGELOU

NO ONE LIKES TO TALK ABOUT WHAT happens when the lights go out—after the kids go to bed and everyone's asleep, the thoughts you are left with, the stress that keeps you tossing and turning, never feeling like you have time to process because your life is too demanding. I cannot tell you how many times I've waited until I was alone to cry so no one would see. When we continue to let the pressure build up without release, it is only a matter of time before the tension reaches a breaking point.

We all have different ideas of what our lives will look like once we are grown. I had always pictured myself as a wife and a mom, but there were no sleepless nights and endless dishes in my story. There was no childhood trauma that would affect the way I loved the ones I cared for most. I had concocted a fairytale that romanticized marriage and children, not understanding the very real work it would all take.

Don't get it twisted. My journey would not have been what it is without my husband and children. They have enriched my life in every way possible, but I had to drop the fairytale ideology. Becoming Her is about freeing yourself from the thoughts and beliefs that hold you back. It's a process of shedding anything that prevents you from fully embracing the beauty of the present moment. No matter how enticing or alluring these thoughts and beliefs may seem, if they hinder you from appreciating what's right in front of you, you must let them go. Stop imagining how your life could be if only and start recognizing and loving what is.

Fear is the leading cause of most of our torment. An overactive fear can create a very real hell. I can't speak for you, but I knew something was up for me when my fear of ruining my children made me feel distant... When I met their innocence with unrelated anger... I could not allow my fears to mess this up—this being their innocence. I couldn't show up for them the way they needed until I dealt with *me*.

I did not want the world to callous my children as it had done me, not realizing that some of my ways of protecting them could create those very same callouses. As I reflected on those times, I realized that I was more concerned with protecting them from my past than loving them in their present. And I know I am not the only one. You've experienced some very real things in your life, but it is not theirs to carry. This not only applies to women with children, but it also applies to every relationship in your life. When you are at war with yourself, the casualties know no end. At a time when I thought I was giving my best, there came a point when that was no longer sufficient.

I believe no one should have to heal from things they never experienced, especially a child. But if you are unaware of what is happening, it is a real possibility. In my community, we talk about generational curses. Pain that is passed down from generation to generation. My lack of awareness about how my trauma affected the way I interacted with the world, most importantly, the impact of my role as a mother, increased the likelihood of passing on or perpetuating a new generational curse.

Good intentions are not enough, at least not for me. I believed (and still believe) my children and my husband deserve more than my good intentions. My good intentions and love for them had to be followed up with good actions. I had to commit to myself that I would release the demons (the pain, the trauma, the hurt) that had a hold on me. These were my demons to fight, not theirs. They should not have to arm up for my battle but would if I continued that path. And I am sure it would have manifested in them having bouts of irrational anger and trouble connecting with and trusting people. This just wasn't an option for me. It was non-negotiable. That's not who I wanted to be for them and, most of all, that isn't who I wanted to be for myself.

Every person standing at a ledge has someone or something there to push them over. I say this metaphorically. I can vividly remember tipping points in my life where I was pushed into the abyss. It was as if all choices were ripped from me, and I had landed in the middle of the sea. For most of my life, I have had to figure that out—figure it out. I figured out so much hard stuff by myself that allowing someone else to be a part of the process almost cost me my marriage. It was ingrained in me to take care of myself, and I did that by any means necessary. And just when I thought I had it all figured out, and it'd be smooth sailing from there, I would be catapulted further into the abyss.

There are glimpses in our lives where we genuinely want to be better, even during the storm. This is true for me, and I believe it to be true for most people. But our conditioning and environments can make that road feel so out of reach, flirting with the idea of doing better in life and taking care of ourselves in a myriad of ways but never deeply committing. Why do you think that is?

Personally, I could commit to becoming physically better with no problem. But the real work that needed to be done—you know, all that inner work with its complexities and trauma—felt like too much. When I considered the situation, my perspective made inner work seem elusive and unimportant, especially when compared to the multitude of distractions and responsibilities that held my focus tightly. This work needed more than I was willing to give, at times, causing me to choose to do nothing. So, in short, there was no time for it; or, at least, I had successfully convinced myself so...that is until I lost the will to live.

So, who pushed me over the edge? What did it?

Life.

Throughout our lives, the choices we make shape the path we walk and define the reality we experience. My decisions, up to this point, had led me to a fairly satisfactory external existence…

Husband.

House.

Child.

Career.

It looked good on the outside.

After losing my babies, life forced me into a new way of being. Losing them took something so precious from me, leaving a void that seemed impossible to fill. However, their absence also propelled me into a journey of self-discovery and introspection. I found myself teetering between holding on to the memories that shaped me and reaching for the deeper meaning behind it all. This delicate balance between reminiscence and seeking understanding became a vital part of my emotional and spiritual growth.

If I am honest, some of the trauma I endured is still kind of a blur. I just know I went into a military setting to seek treatment from people I had deemed the enemy. My therapist was a young white woman, who I felt could not help me. How could she relate to me? She was young, and she was white. I was wrong. It was not what she said but what she did.

Being in a therapy session was the first time someone held space for me to just release. I am pretty sure most days I simply cried, and she comforted me. The doctors wanted to prescribe me medicine, but I declined. It was like my pain was what kept me close to my babies. If I let that go, would I be letting them go too?

I didn't feel like I deserved to be happy. I did not receive any support from my military leadership either. They actually wanted me to come back after fourteen days because physically I would be fit to work. That is when I knew I would not be making a career out of the US Air Force because, to them, I am just another number. It was an experience I would not wish on a soul.

Mentally, I was broken. Being so casually discounted was the final, most devastating blow to my already fragile self-image and worth. I kept finding myself at a point of thinking, *It can't get worse than this,* and then it did. Losing my beautiful baby boy and girl, and how I was treated after, is what sent me over the edge.

Consider this: Saying goodbye before you're ready does something to you, especially when it comes to your child. The goodbye feels permanent. There was a numbness that came over me, and there were days when I wished I had fought harder for them. If we would have died together, so be it. *Yeah, I had those days.* Those were the darker moments I mostly battled alone. Unsettled grief can be a slow suicide.

The twins' death cracked something in me, and it got really dark before I even considered the light. Spending nearly a week in the hospital, fighting to save their lives, fighting to save me, and losing was not where I wanted to be yet I never would have thought it might be the catalyst for such drastic changes. They sent me on a journey to find out how to love myself, despite what I thought I knew and believed I deserved. They made me question who I was and what I was doing in this life.

Before the twins, I was mostly living unconsciously. I'm not entirely certain I would have ever found the motivation to confront and work through all the emotional pain and brokenness I had been carrying inside of me if it weren't for them. For that, I am grateful. I may have never found the courage to forgive myself for things that were never in my control to begin with. Although I still have glimpses of what life would have been like if they were here, I can't change what happened that day, but I did choose to grow from it.

This is not where I act like it didn't hurt because it did and still does. I still weep for my babies, but I have found joy in the time we shared. It is because of them that I began to look at my soil before planting more seeds. The seeds they got to plant in me have continued to blossom over the years, and I now have the opportunity to encourage and empower other people—particularly women—to make the choice to grow towards the person they want to become.

Before losing them, I was already battling with understanding who I was. The Black female experience is altogether different straight from the womb—professionally, maternally, relationally, educationally, and financially. You name it, and it's never the same for us. Being a Black woman can be physically and mentally taxing, as well as emotionally draining without everything else life throws at us. And, many times, because some of us are focused on being the best at all things, all the time, we don't develop a real relationship with ourselves. This struggle isn't exclusive to Black women; it is a common experience shared by women all over the world. I just kept showing up for everybody else, and I had no idea what truly loving me even looked or felt like. And I had spent a good majority of my time before this looking for someone else to do the job for me. I discovered there were a lot of things I had learned to accept and things about myself I didn't know—emotional wounds I thought I would never address.

As a child, I would pray to forget all the bad things that happened in life. I grew up listening to this song called

"Amnesia" by Cherish, and I yearned to forget when the real answer was to forgive. (I learned that later.) I finally began to realize willful ignorance and neglect did not lead me to eternal bliss but instead into a constant battle with myself. For many years, I carried the belief that the most painful aspect of my being was the hurt from my past, and as a result, I tried to avoid confronting it. Little did I realize that by turning away from it, I was inadvertently allowing the shadow of my past to loom larger over my life. It wasn't until I made a conscious effort to make peace with myself that I began to understand the impact of this avoidance.

Forgiveness is a journey. While many of us have experience forgiving others, we can all work on learning how to forgive ourselves. Learning to forgive myself created a freedom I had never known. I have reached a point in my life where I refuse to let unforgiveness and feelings of guilt or shame control how I perceive my own value and worth.

If there is something in your past or present that you are holding on to, and it's causing you to feel small or undeserving, it's important to acknowledge it and work towards forgiveness. If you are coping with a major loss, I can't tell you how to grieve or when to stop. I just know that hiding was no longer an option for me. The unbearable pain forced me to look, to feel, and to be uncomfortable. Ultimately, it made me stronger, and I want the same for you.

INVITATION:
Holding Space for You

The odds that you've experienced some type of pain in your life, and you are reading this is probably 1000%. The extent of that pain will vary. You don't have to experience an astronomical loss for you to begin doing self-work. Something I had to learn was not to allow anyone to tell me how badly something hurt or didn't hurt or the effect it had on me.

The experience of pain is a natural and important part of being human. While pain can be difficult to endure, it serves as a signal that something is wrong and needs attention. Acknowledging the pain allows you to take steps to address its cause and to work towards finding relief. It's a reminder that your well-being is worth fighting for and that you have the strength and resilience to overcome. Therefore, the exercises below have been created for you to build a new relationship with parts of you that feel more tender from the pain you've experienced. Once again, this is not about getting it right but allowing yourself to heal.

STEP 1: MAKE ROOM
- Sit or lie down in a comfortable position. Close your eyes if you feel comfortable doing so.
- Begin by taking slow, deep breaths. Inhale deeply through your nose, hold for a few seconds, and exhale slowly through your mouth.
- Focus on your breath, allowing it to bring you into the present moment. Feel the rise and fall of your chest with each breath.

STEP 2: REFLECTIVE JOURNALING
- Open a journal or notebook and answer the following prompts:
  - What is the weight you carry that no one else sees?
  - Why has it been yours to carry?

- Do you have to carry it alone?
- How has pain (loss, grief, sorrow) shaped your relationship with yourself?

STEP 3: VALIDATING YOUR PAIN

- Take some time to write a heartfelt and compassionate letter to yourself. Validate your own feelings and acknowledge the emotions you are or have experienced. Use phrases like:
    - "I acknowledge that you have experienced deep emotional pain, and it is valid."
    - "My feelings and reactions are important and deserve attention."
    - "It's okay to feel hurt, and it's okay to take the time you need to heal."

STEP 4: REST AND REFLECT

Spend a few moments in stillness, allowing your body and mind to absorb the experience.

Give it a day or so and come back to it. Read it, continue to allow yourself to develop compassion for the person who has walked this earth carrying the burdens of past mistakes, regrets, abuse, and neglect, and be with that person because they need you more than anyone else.

This level of vulnerability and openness may feel intimidating because it requires confronting deep-seated emotions and burdens you've been carrying. It's crucial to dedicate time to self-care, self-discovery, and self-love. Seeking the support of a therapist or a coach is highly advisable. They have played a crucial role in saving many lives, including mine, by providing guidance, empathy, and effective coping strategies.

chapter 11
Unforgivable

"If you are silent about your pain, they'll kill you and say you enjoyed it."

—ZORA NEALE HURSTON

Everyone needs a therapist.

THIS IS SOMETHING I HEARD FROM MANY people before I actually sought one out. People told me how amazing therapy is and the relief it would provide, and while this is true, there is also a ton of pain that is felt during the journey toward relief. Nevertheless, after losing the twins, I went straight into therapy—not by choice, but because folks knew, at any moment, I could checkout because life felt meaningless.

My experience in Alaska was forever tainted, and we cut our time there short. We headed back to the east coast to be closer to family living on the mainland—starting with life on a new base, a new pot. Do you think I continued my therapy? *No.* I spent maybe one month in sessions after losing the twins, and while it was very beneficial, it didn't even scratch the surface.

Five months into being stationed in Delaware, we found out we were pregnant again. My body still carried the weight of the twins physically, mentally, and emotionally. And as excited as I was, I was equally scared out of my mind. The what-ifs rang loud, and I knew I couldn't do it alone. More than that, I didn't want to do it alone. So, I sought out a new therapist, this time on my own.

Remember in a previous chapter when I told you it doesn't matter if other people tell you your pot stinks and has holes, you must be the one to acknowledge it? Well, my soil was reeking, and I didn't want it to infect the new bundle of joy we were bringing into the world. I needed to fix all my cracks, and I needed to do it before another flower sprang up.

This new therapist had no idea what she was getting herself into. *Poor her.* Every secret I never spoke aloud was shared. Everything I was hiding behind my walls began to overflow, and I felt like I had been hit by a train—emotionally and physically. To say I felt like a trainwreck was the least; during that season, I may have been *the* trainwreck.

We spoke about things I had never trusted myself to tell, like the experiences where I was taken advantage of. Because

I told no one and blamed myself, I carried those secrets in the depths of my soul. I began to recognize the seeds of mistrust I'd planted within me as a child. I learned not to trust myself or my own judgment…that someone else knew better. It was easier this way, I believed. I was weak and will forever require 'being saved' is the lie I chose.

I want to pause here for accuracy and intentionality. I am not telling you this story for your sympathy. And I understand it will invoke some strong responses from many people. You may even see yourself in my story. That thing you are feeling right now is called connection. It's something I find people shy away from. Don't stop here. Don't get stuck. I want you to lean in and remember this feeling. Nurture it. My vulnerability, *your* vulnerability, allows people to connect with you. The same thing you are fighting so hard to hide is the same thing that will connect you to your soul tribe. I am not speaking from theory but from my lived experience and the beautiful relationships I have cultivated in this life.

We will get into that later. For now, let's finish what we started.

As I shared earlier, therapy saved my life and the lives of others I know personally. Use this time and make space for your healing. This will look different to each of us, and grace and trust are going to be necessary. Grant it to yourself and be open to all it yields, as you pen your next chapter.

My entire life, I have heard about unconditional love, but honestly, I never knew what it truly meant. And while this love sounded amazing, it was not the type of love I experienced regularly. The love I had become familiar with was laced with conditions. It was a journey that took me a considerable amount of time to truly acknowledge and embrace myself, seeing myself through my own eyes and through the eyes of God.

For too long I found myself second-guessing what I was doing, saying, or even wearing. I used to place my self-worth in the hands of others, allowing them to determine my value based on their opinions and actions. This made me feel vulnerable and at the mercy of their acceptance or rejection. By loving in this way, I unintentionally gave away my power and allowed others to influence how I felt about myself. It took me a while to realize that this behavior stemmed from low self-worth because that's never what I outwardly showed.

Instead, I overcompensated with false confidence, humor, and sarcasm (yup, a true New Yorker). This deep-rooted belief that there was something wrong with me caused me to believe everything I had control of would fail. Somehow, because I was tainted, I would mess up any and everything I touched. (Hence why I gave my control away so easily.) Abdicating my power led me into relationships with people who could take advantage of this docile version of me.

Faith is a powerful force that influences our lives more than we may realize. Our deepest beliefs have the ability to shape our reality, whether we are conscious of it or not. I will say that as many times as needed until it becomes ingrained into your mind. When we hold onto beliefs that are not aligned with our desires, we can find ourselves feeling trapped in a victim mentality, unable to break free from negative patterns and experiences. Life does not have to happen to you; it can happen *for you*. This mindset shift has been key to my growth. I am not going to act like it is easy or the easiest outlook to adopt, especially when you have experienced a considerable amount of trauma. But after losing the twins and blaming myself, for getting up and going to PT, for not being a good enough wife/mother/daughter—you fill in your blank—I had to make a decision.

What's yours?

I changed my "Why me God?" mantra to "What's here for me, God?"

We lost the twins on our fifth wedding anniversary. Twenty percent of marriages end in divorce during the first five years; add that to the bereavement of losing children and still never dealing with childhood wounds and trauma. We did not know what we were in for from the moment we said, "I do." There were times of uncertainty along the way, times when I felt more 'I don't,' but it had less to do with marriage and more to do with the mirage I'd set in motion… Tired of feeling hopeless. Tired of looking for someone to save me…fix me. To make me better, make me worth it.

I had to figure it out on my own. The smoke had no intention of clearing by itself, so I needed to do it for myself.

I need you to understand no one is coming. You need to do it for yourself. Trust and support have taken my healing to another level. I had to learn how to trust myself and others to seek help. Much of what I learned about myself came from sharing with other people I trusted enough to open up to. Growth involves moving past embarrassment and speaking your truth so freely that someone capable of supporting you can do so effectively. If you live a lie, people will support that lie. If you live in truth, people will love and support the real you. It's that simple.

There's a saying that if something isn't growing, it's dying. The saying suggests that if something is not actively developing or improving in the natural order of things, it is likely to decline or perish. Are you growing? Are you taking everything you've been through to push you towards purpose? Or are you making excuses on why you can't or aren't able to be the woman you desire? Nobody has to live or die with that decision but you. However, I hope you choose growth because you deserve it.

Hear me... We are not born cold or callous. We were not born sarcastic or critical, and we were not born doubting ourselves or our abilities. No, we learned those things and not by ourselves. That's why I don't think some of the heavy lifting of healing can be done alone. Once you begin to realize the beliefs you hold and the voices in your head are not your truth, you will be able to separate them from who you truly are and who you are becoming. Yes, some of the things you've learned are from the very people you've loved and still love. But just as you can learn something that breaks you, you can learn something that builds you. Creating a community and support will allow you to rest easier, knowing that you truly are not alone.

I've had the incredible privilege of organizing and leading workshops for women in diverse locations across the globe. It's truly inspiring to see women from all walks of life coming together, united in their quest for deeper understanding and purpose. Occasionally, I encounter individuals who initially join without a clear understanding of what to expect, only to leave profoundly transformed by the experience. The calling that was happening in them on a subconscious level was to sisterhood. One of the most cherished aspects for many participants is the opportunity to listen to other women share their personal stories and valuable insights. Witnessing the support and celebration of women by others is something that cannot be duplicated if you're trying to heal all alone.

INVITATION:
Creating Your Safe Spaces

In the last chapter, we discussed how therapy and community saved me, shifted my perspective, and how I now use it to help other women shift theirs as well. So, this invitation is all about you building your community. It is designed to move you from awareness to action. Take your time with it, but don't procrastinate because what you are looking for is waiting for you to find it.

Step 1: Reflecting on Your Current Support System
- **List Your Support System:**
  - Take a piece of paper or your notebook/journal and list out the people in your life who currently support you. This could include family, friends, colleagues, mentors, and/or support groups.

- **List How They Support You:**
  - Next to each person's name, write down how they support you. This could be through emotional support, practical help, advice, companionship, or any other form of encouragement.

Step 2: Reflecting on the Impact of Your Support System
- **Positive Impact:**
  - Reflect on how each person's support has helped you. Write a few sentences about the positive impact they have had on your life. For example, "My friend Sarah listens to me without judgment, which helps me feel understood and valued."
- **Areas for Improvement:**
  - Identify any areas where you feel you need more support. Write down specific situations or feelings where you felt unsupported or alone. For example, "I need more support with managing stress at work."

STEP 3: IDENTIFYING GAPS AND OPPORTUNITIES FOR GROWTH
- **Where You Need More Support:**
  - Look at the areas where you need more support and think about the types of support that could help. This might include emotional support, practical help, social connections, or professional guidance.
- **Potential Community Connections:**
  - Brainstorm ways to expand your community to fill these gaps. This could involve joining an organization or a group, seeking out a mentor, attending networking events, or reaching out to new people. Write down specific actions you can take to push yourself out of your comfort zone and build new connections.

STEP 4: TAKING ACTION TO BUILD YOUR COMMUNITY
- **Action Plan:**
  - Create a simple action plan with steps you can take to build and expand your support network.

  For example:
    - Join a local book club or hobby group.
    - Attend a community event or workshop.
    - Reach out to a colleague or an acquaintance for coffee.
    - Volunteer for a cause you care about to meet like-minded people.
- **Set Small Goals:**
  - Set small, achievable goals to start expanding your community. For example:
    - Commit to attending one new event each month.
    - Reaching out to one new person each week.

STEP 5: REFLECT AND ADJUST
- **Regular Check-ins:**
  - Set aside time regularly to reflect on your progress. Are you feeling more supported? Have you made new connections? What has been challenging? What has been rewarding?
- **Adjust Your Plan:**
  - Based on your reflections, adjust your action plan as needed. Be patient with yourself and recognize that building a support system takes time and effort.
  - This exercise encourages you to create a safe space for self-reflection, to assess your current support system, to identify areas where you need more support, and to take measurable, actionable steps that expand your community.

By pushing yourself out of your comfort zone, you can build a stronger, more supportive network that enhances your well-being and increases your resilience.

chapter 12
Loving from My Hurt Space

"Healing begins where the wound was made."
—ALICE WALKER

THERE'S A SAYING IN MANY PULPITS across the world that we may be "bruised but never broken." Up until to this point, I followed that belief. However, today I would like to make a new statement, one I believe to be truer for me: I was broken and bruised. And not just one time but many times over, and I can accept that. I had to be completely broken down in some areas of my life to truly begin to understand what faith was and is for me. Just as in the pruning of a tree or a plant, something had to break off in order for the strongest, most beautiful parts to appear.

I was no longer just changing pots. I had turned over my soil, and new life was beginning.

The thing about being broken is understanding what it has done and is doing for you, if you allow it. If you're reading this right now and you feel broken, know there is something beautiful on the other side for you, if you choose it. Many of my clients, who are at this point, say things like, "I have no right to complain," and to that, I say, "WRONG!" If your body, mind, and spirit are not happy listen to them. Or live life in resentment—something I know about.

Throughout our lives, we are given signs and indicators that show us what is for us and what is against us. It's the voice that says, "He's not good for you," or "Don't go that way." Something, usually feels off. Your innate knowing can be a subtle whisper like "girl," or it can scream, "GIRL." If you ignore those warnings long enough, they begin to fade into the background noise, never leaving you, but are less and less audible because of willful ignorance. *Yup, I said it.* You're being willfully ignorant of the voice inside of you.

If you're always looking for an exit, you're never really in the room. And that is how I functioned—there but never really present. One thing about me is I always had a Plan B. My Plan B was not created from intuition but always out of survival. My nervous system could not operate in a place where it felt dependent (i.e., relationships, jobs). I needed to know that if, for any reason, this were to fail, I would be better than okay. Now, I fully support the idea of knowing and loving yourself enough so that your world doesn't fall apart when things don't go as planned, such as when someone leaves you or you lose a job. It is what I get to work with women on daily. However, this process is a journey when you've conditioned yourself to operate in survival mode. At this time, I wasn't approaching things from that perspective. Instead, I was preparing for the worst while slightly hoping for the best. And that's not possible. I don't care what anyone says.

Just like you get what you believe you deserve, you also get what you prepare for. And if that's nothing, then you get nothing. And when it happens just as you prepared, you can then say, "Look, I told you." It's a vicious cycle that you've created.

Whenever a partner would confirm my existing suspicion with any activity that supported my Plan B, I would be like, "See, yup that's why I move like I move."

That's not right, but it was survival for me. I was loudly independent and silently lonely and afraid... Afraid of what it would mean if I truly trusted that someone could love me as I am.

You see, love is not just a word; it is a practice. And just like any practice, it depends on what you have learned. Your current practice in love may be more detrimental than it is helpful, like mine was. Taking the time to step back and evaluate where you love from and how you love is going to be a game-changer. I am not just saying this, I mean it. I loved from my hurt space for a long time, and it cost me a lot.

Not knowing who you are can cause a ton of pain and hurt, too—not just to others, but mostly to yourself. I did not realize that I would attract love solely from my hurt space. I believe in favor because I know my story could be so much worse. The decisions I made from not feeling like enough did not always put me in the safest predicaments. The hardest part was healing and teaching the people who became an integral part of my life prior who I am now that the healing has begun. When someone is used to loving you when you're broken, it can be difficult for them to understand how to love you when you come back to the realization that you are whole.

Case in point...

Previously, people knew me to be a certain way, and when I embarked on this journey, I got to introduce them to me—the real me, the me I choose to be now. This wasn't always conducive to their relationship with me. So, I had to learn the art of letting go. Not the "oh, I am done with you forever, get out of my face, and I ain't got time for you" kind, but just allowing space for my growth to create a natural separation. When you're on a healing journey, your very presence—be it on social media or in real life—will irritate a lot of people, typically the unhealed. You will not have to cut them off; they won't want to be bothered with you, and that's okay. I am not saying it may not hurt but learn to understand that they are on a journey, too. We all are, whether growth happens or not.

Which brings me here…

When we take things personally, nine times out of ten, there is an insecurity or a wound of some sort. So, when this scab gets agitated by someone saying or doing something, we're simply not upset about that moment. We are likely angry from whenever and wherever the pain originated, say nine years old. That is your hurt space. In my case, that's 25 years of pent-up aggression or brokenness.

How old are you? Do you take most things personally?

Here's why it hurts so much. Because, it's an open wound that has never been resolved. Instead, it's been festering.

They say an addict doesn't get a reset…that no matter how long they've been clean, if they start using again, they will pick up where they left off. That's because the body keeps score. I was addicted to my pain because it gave me the excuse I needed to not live the life I had always wanted—the one God ordained. It allowed me to settle and stay comfortable even if the comfort caused me more pain. It was the pain I knew, the pain I was willing to endure.

We become hypnotized by the everyday familiar pain we know, and we call it living. Thus, marriage has become one of my best teachers. The patience my husband has with me is God-sent. Because, if I was dealing with a me for fourteen years? I don't know... *Shout out to you, Bae!* But in all seriousness, we've learned a lot from each other. I can remember when I would get so wrapped up in the heat of the moment that I become fully engrossed—in full battle mode—trying to be right about something I honestly don't even care about. I have learned to move past being right and opening my world to where my emotions are pointing me. Why was I fighting so hard, or why was I so reluctant? When I paused to find that thing—whether it be in the conversation or later on—that is where I could have an open conversation about what is really real for me and why. This can be tough because even though you may understand the source of your pain, the other person doesn't always know. Still, being able to feel it, to give it words, and to express it from a place where you feel safe will change everything.

I am a firm believer that if you don't learn a lesson that is sent to you, it will keep coming back around until you get it. But each time it comes around, the consequence of not getting the lesson becomes graver and graver. Loving from your hurt space can only create more hurt. Hurt people attract hurt people. And just because someone is hurting doesn't mean they're not funny and kind with a gazillion other great attributes. It simply begs to differ that when they don't have access to those "warm and fuzzy" feelings when they are triggered, who then do they become? A better statement is, they become someone else.

It's great to know a person when they're happy, but you don't truly know a person until you experience them when they're down, and the shadow emotions emerge. If you choose to love from your hurt space, you run the risk of continuing in a cycle that leaves you empty, tired, and feeling stuck. It's like when you date a new person but the same person. It's the friendships that always end the same. It's the feeling that everyone is using you, and you can't catch a break. If you have experienced this or are currently experiencing this, it's time to choose differently. It's time to stop accepting less from others, but most importantly yourself. No more surviving, it's your time to thrive.

INVITATION:
Where Are You Loving From?

Allow yourself to go through these exercises with an openness, knowing it will only deepen your relationship with yourself.

Reflective Journaling Prompts

Spend a few minutes reflecting on and writing down your responses to the following prompts:

- **Recent Conflicts:**
    - Think about a recent conflict or an argument you had in a close relationship. Describe the situation in detail.
    - What emotions did you feel during the conflict? Were there feelings of insecurity, fear, or past hurts that surfaced?

- **Triggers and Reactions:**
    - Identify specific triggers in your relationships that cause strong emotional reactions. Are these reactions tied to past hurts or traumas?
    - How do you typically respond to these triggers? Are your responses more defensive, aggressive, or avoidant?

Patterns in Relationships:

Reflect on any patterns you notice in your relationships. Do you often feel unappreciated, misunderstood, or insecure? Are there recurring themes or issues that seem to arise in multiple relationships?

Positive Moments:

Think about positive, loving moments in your relationships. How do you feel during these times? Are you able to fully enjoy and appreciate these moments, or do you feel a sense of unease or doubt?

Self-Perception:

How do you view yourself in your relationships? Do you feel worthy of love and respect, or do you often doubt your value and worthiness?

BODY AWARENESS EXERCISE:
1. Sit comfortably and close your eyes. Take several deep breaths, focusing on relaxing your body.
2. Slowly scan your body from head to toe, paying attention to areas where you feel tension, discomfort, or pain. These physical sensations can be indicators of emotional stress or unresolved issues.
3. As you identify these areas, ask yourself if they might be related to emotional hurts or past traumas that are affecting your current relationships.

VISUALIZATION:

Envision two versions of yourself: One that is loving from a place of hurt and another that is loving from a place of healing.

Hurt Self:
1. Picture how you act and feel when you are loving from your hurt self. What behaviors, thoughts, and emotions are present?
2. How do you interact with others? What kind of energy do you bring into your relationships?

Healed Self:
1. Now, visualize yourself loving from a healed, whole place. What behaviors, thoughts, and emotions characterize this version of you?
2. How do you interact with others? What kind of energy do you bring into your relationships?
3. Compare the two versions of yourself and note the differences.

ACTION STEPS:

Based on your reflections and visualizations, write down specific actions you can take to move past loving from a hurt place to loving from a healed place. Examples might include:
- Seeking therapy or counseling to address past traumas.
- Practicing self-care and self-compassion regularly
- Communicating openly and honestly with loved ones about your feelings and needs
- Setting healthy boundaries to protect your emotional well-being
- Engaging in activities that promote healing and personal growth, such as meditation, journaling, or joining support groups.

COMMITMENT TO HEALING:

Write a commitment statement to yourself. This could be something like, "I commit to healing my past hurts and learning to love from a place of wholeness and strength. I deserve healthy, fulfilling relationships and will take the necessary steps to achieve this."

chapter 13
Ungrateful

"Fear is only inverted faith; it is faith in evil instead of good."

—FLORENCE SCOVEL SHINN

I GREW UP IN A DEVOUT, CHRISTIAN HOME. My grandfather moved from Florida in the 1940s to start a church. So, when I say we were in church twenty-four-seven, we were in church twenty-four-ten.

Church holds a lot of memories in my head and heart. As children, we never questioned what we had learned; we just learned it. For the longest time, I was okay with being told what and how to believe. To be honest, it made life easy. It took away responsibility and accountability. For instance, "I'm just doing what they told me." But I didn't have faith in my ability to choose or do the right thing for me.

Miriam dictionary defines faith as certitude even where there is no evidence or proof. As a child, I watched adults wail and cry and talk about how good God was while in church and how He could do anything. Yet when the doors of those churches closed behind them, I watched the fear and overwhelm begin to creep in until they got their next fix of faith the following Sunday and it was on wash, rinse, repeat. I watched this play out not only in church but in life in general.

Faith goes beyond religion. And the reason I want to share with you where my faith began is to paint a picture of how it has evolved. I don't believe faith is not what we see modeled before us day-to-day. Fear is the common practice and not far behind it is resentment... For the chances not taken, the words not spoken, the time lost—all because of choosing to practice fear over faith. (I'll speak for myself.) No matter how much I read about this supernatural power, I did not trust it. I needed to control what I could see, allowing fear to dictate what I did and didn't do. I was unfaithful. I did not truly believe anyone or anything could do anything outside of me, and that leaked onto everything I touched.

For me, faith is intimate. It is a relationship that needs to be developed. I don't believe it can be taught; it must be felt… experienced…on so many levels. You may have witnessed it in other people's lives, but someone else's faith cannot be transferred to you. It is an experience that can inspire you if you let it, but it is a gift you must be able to tap into within the power of you.

After losing the twins, my faith in the unseen and the unknown increased tenfold. In the beginning, I was clinging to the hope that there was meaning in this loss. But, eventually, it led to a much further and deeper understanding of what it means to know with certainty "everything is working for my good."

I read the book *The Game of Life and How to Play It* by Florence Scovel Shinn. In her book, she made a statement that has stuck with me, "Fear is only inverted faith." *Mind blown.* Why? Because, it means it's already in you.

I had always looked at fear and faith separately, independent of one another. Moving forward with Florence's interpretation meant that the shift from faith to fear happens based on what you choose to believe. We spoke in earlier chapters about getting what you prepare for. Well, fear dwells in the belief that nothing is possible, while faith dwells in ALL things are possible. The obvious choice would be the latter, but is it the practiced choice? Is it what you've been practicing?

I finally figured out where I was going all wrong. I saw and practiced faith from a supernatural standpoint, but I saw and practiced fear in the natural. Fear was more practiced and, in return, became normalized and easy to access. The same can be done for faith. Let's begin to normalize things working out for your good, too.

Believing, in faith, that everything will work out for you is intimidating when you're pulling from your database full of disappointments and failures. I am not here to invalidate your experiences… Disappointment hurts. But it also can save you from situations that would have been detrimental to you and to your life. Those are the moments when you think, *Thank God, I dodged that bullet.*

It is all in what you practice.

Likewise, I am no stranger to tears. I have cried over things that never belonged to me. I once craved my pain because it was the thing that reminded me I was alive. So, I've got some history of being willfully intentional, which is exactly what I needed—to be intentional about letting go of my pain and leaning more into the belief that it is all working out for me.

My favorite tree is a weeping willow. My husband calls them the sad tree, and every time I would get offended because, to me, they're the most beautiful tree in the world. As I began to learn more about the weeping willow, I discovered that every part of the tree, from its stringy branches to where they decided to plant themselves, is intentional too. This time, it's you who needs to have faith and be intentional about where you're planted.

Now, how many times have you heard be grateful or show gratitude, and everything will begin to shift in your life? Yeah, me too. And I am here to intentionally call BS—not because I don't believe that gratitude can't shift everything in your life, because it can. But starting a gratitude journal in the midst of your storm, where your negative thoughts and energy are overpowering you daily, just isn't enough. You must also feel it for faith to work.

I knew I had much to be grateful for, but I could not *feel* it. (The key word here is feel.) Therefore, faith in me messing things up prevailed.

When I can *feel* gratefulness in my body, I know the gratitude experience to be true. I know the faith experience to be real. However, I could ramble out things I was grateful for and still struggle through the day, trying to remain positive when I didn't. My faith was holding; I was just not being very intentional about where I directed it. There was something in my soil that needed to be sifted, and I was just waking up to the idea that there was a correlation between my fears and my faith. I could not feel grateful or practice gratitude to the magnitude in which it should be practiced until I understood and believed I was deserving enough of all the beautiful things in my life and stopped being afraid. I needed to be intentional about feeling worthy internally and not just knowing, aimlessly hoping because knowing and experiencing are on different ends of the spectrum.

How could I get there? How could I start to internalize gratitude for myself? And, even greater, how could I make myself believe? From where would my faith come?

Like me, you *can't* skip steps—particularly this one. I mean you could, but it feels kind of hopeless when you do. And *that* is the opposite of faith. At your core, you need to know you are ready to immerse yourself into the wisdom (knowing) and being (feeling) of the freedom you deserve.

Just like faith can't be taught, gratitude can't be planted into your heart and grow into the immense tree it supposed to be if your soil is bad. It doesn't work. Trust me. I've tried. And I am trying to spare you the heartache and the possibility of blaming yourself (or others). Gratitude, like faith, is an experience, too.

It is a practice, and before you practice anything, you must understand your why? Asking this does not cause the question to magically disappear—releasing all doubt, anger, disgust, unfulfillment, and general unhappiness—when you know you should be grateful or feel grateful. Still, I have good news and good news! The answer is YOU and YOU.

Why is forgiving ourselves so hard? I am not here to play judge and jury or to even tell you what to believe, think or feel. It took me a while to figure out that it does not have to be this way. Through my journey, I have learned we were granted unlimited forgiveness the moment we came into this world. It is what the world has taught you otherwise; it's why we don't *feel* free. You must stop punishing yourself. It is time to stop packing salt into your self-inflicted wounds. You are the only person who has the power to allow yourself to be forgiven— truly, freely forgiven. We choose to walk around feeling guilty about our past mistakes, and sometimes other people may play a part, too. But, ultimately, it is up to you!

What I am suggesting for you is to forget what you've been trained to believe about forgiveness—about grace and *faith*. I know you're probably like, "Laniece, how in the world can I do that? I have been indoctrinated into this system where guilt and unforgiveness is served up as a side dish and the main course." But, it doesn't have to be. We must learn how to give ourselves grace and space (remember?) to evolve into who we are meant to be. Our self-criticisms will cripple any progression and keep us in a place where we will continue to feel unforgivable. Start small. Begin by allowing yourself to acknowledge that "yes, you have made a mistake," but today simply is a new day! And every new day is a chance to do and to be better!

As I stated earlier, I am not here to judge you, but I am also not here to provide you with amnesty. What I can offer you from experience is the knowledge of forgiving yourself. So let me start here: I don't care what you've done or when you've done it! That does not matter to me. Know that we cannot move forward until we forgive ourselves for whatever act we believe has been our undoing. *In faith*, it is time for you to heal from that place and to move toward the person you were designed to be, the person waiting for you to become *Her*.

Are you ready? I can help you.

From my own experience, there was no true healing until I acknowledged I was still holding on to guilt from long ago. I wore my unforgiveness as a permanent badge of disgrace, never fully understanding why. And, to be honest, for the longest I had bonded myself to my negative outlook on life and never thought to question it. This was my norm: Operating in fear.

Bringing ourselves to understand the why in our lives can take time. It is not something we should try to rush through, but instead use every opportunity to address. For example, when something happens in your day that causes you to react negatively—whether an angry outburst, sarcasm, or even shutting down—these are the perfect opportunities to get to the root of your why.

Why are you reacting this way? What is really bothering you? You can ask yourself these questions a million times until you get to a point where you feel ready to move through it. Once you reach this place of no longer believing whatever it is that caused you to react negatively, then can you move toward the how:

1. How can I feel this overwhelming sense of guilt? Consider where it is coming from.
2. How can I heal from it? Consider where you are going.

I will be honest. Depending on how deep your issues lie, if you have not yet sought therapy, I recommend doing it now. Therapy is a great resource to begin to help you work through issues that stem from past trauma. It provides a safe space to say things you have never spoken aloud. And the biggest bonus is, unlike friends and family, this person is legally bound not to go run and tell your business. They are also highly trained to work through your specific problems with you.

This is a suggestion, but not a law. Start where you feel comfortable, but check in with yourself to recognize if you need additional help. Okay? Okay.

chapter 14
Unspoken

"Your silence will not protect you."

—AUDRE LORDE

IT IS OFTEN UNSPOKEN TRUTHS THAT hold us captive. They are the things about us we try to run so far away from that we don't even realize we're running in circles. And no matter how big that circle gets, until the truth is spoken…until it's seen…you will continue to run.

Some of us didn't choose walls; we simply gave up on this life because other humans can really be brutal. And when you are not at a space in life where you can understand that hurt people, hurt people, then the hurt and pain they caused you can make this life seem unbearably miserable. I've been there, and I thank God I'm not there now. Still, I know what it's like to be there, and I know how isolating it can feel when all you really want is to be accepted—to be heard, seen, understood and loved. I know I am not the first person to say this to you, but only you can grant yourself the acceptance you seek.

The best of us pretend, and some even quit. But for those of us who do pretend, the cracks begin to show... The building is unstable; it is coming down. Or, we get lost in deep waters, and our legs and arms can no longer keep us afloat. We grab for anything that can help us hold on—career, relationship, the PTA, social media or social clubs—any kind of attention, alcohol, drugs, food. *Pick your poison.* We mistake it for our life jacket instead of escapism.

Where is our life jacket? How do you ask to be saved when no one can see that you're drowning, especially when things don't look so bad from the outside?

We usually don't, and we slip further and further away into the abyss of what feels like nothingness because it's comfortable; it's familiar. For every external accomplishment, for every event, for every celebration, we internally unplug and disconnect from our very being.

So, how do we find our way out? We go in. The military had a saying I hated "Embrace the suck." Why would I ever want to do that? What I think they meant in their ineloquent way is we must learn to embrace the chaos. We must go inward to do the hard work. We get to take care of ourselves, learn ourselves, love ourselves...

I'm here to tell you no one, or nothing will be able to solve that aching or void you feel or have felt. You deserve the time and effort it will take to begin healing, so do it. This starts with admitting that everything is not "fine" and acknowledging you don't need to push through any more pain. You can simply choose to accept it and begin releasing it. The pain that you feel when you look at your situation comes from resisting the reality of what is. Instead, you get caught up in feelings of "if only" and "this shouldn't be happening," making you feel as though things should be different. But when you begin to accept things and see them as they are, you can see openings for something new and potentially better. Free your mind from wishing for a new reality and, instead, see all the possibilities that lie before you.

Admitting to yourself "I am not where I want to be, but I am far from where I've been, and I am open to learning more" can help move you from resistance into a place of flow. However, I have learned honesty is always the starting point. It's okay to say the very thing I wished for is also incredibly hard for me, like marriage and kids at one time. I got tired. I didn't want to do it my way anymore or on my own. I wanted to be better for myself and for them.

Many of the women I work with and know struggle with trust for valid reasons. When you're violated physically, emotionally, psychologically or spiritually, it can become difficult to trust again, but I beg you to learn to open your heart because there are people who want to love you. They've been waiting to do so. People who were sent on your journey to help you heal, to help you trust not only them but you… People like me!

There are people operating in this world with a special gift. I am calling it a gift because it's just misdirected (and it is something I used to do). There are people who can make other people feel close to them when, in reality, they're a world away. That's the thing with pretending; you become really, really, really good at it. And that will have you in a room full of people, feeling all alone. Even with the little people you've created—the ones you love most—there can be a silent distance created by all the things that have been unspoken, untended. If this isn't you, and your life is perfect, YESSS! But if this is you in any way, shape or form, there is a way forward.

I truly believe we never fully know ourselves, and even when we think we've got it, we evolve. It's called awareness. Once I began this journey to self-love and awareness, I was on a euphoric high. It felt like I could finally see myself and the world. I felt I could conquer anything.

This is the part of me I discovered once I left the military. It was 2017 when my husband and I both got tasked to deploy, and I decided it was time to chuck up the deuces. No way would I be leaving my kids with someone for six or seven months. So, I stayed back while my husband went.

That is when it began to happen. I evolved.

Taking some tough looks at myself, I knew I needed to focus. I was working on my master's degree but wasn't mastering me. I wasn't even taking care of myself. It is hard to take care of someone you barely know.

A question I often ask my clients in the beginning of our sessions is what makes you happy? And often they have no idea or no real depth to what truly makes them happy. I know that feeling because it is exactly what I had experienced. I was just moving from one accomplishment to the next, one kid activity to the next, overly wrapped up in meeting the expectations of others—joy or no joy. And let's be honest about expectations. They are often never spoken yet always implied in a relationship where communication is not constantly worked on. I can honestly say I made my own life harder by believing I had to be and do certain things because I thought it was what was expected of me. I thought it was what made my husband or children or parents happy. My own thoughts created a *happy* little prison for me to do things I didn't really want to do and never say things I really wanted to say. If this is you right now, and you are aware of it, trust me… You can break these habits. If this is you, and you're just becoming aware of it after reading this passage, give yourself grace and space.

I want to make this abundantly clear: I do not believe we completely rid ourselves of every "bad" habit. I instead believe we become more aware of them and in each moment we have a choice to make. Each new choice leads to a different outcome, one where you hopefully start a better habit. But, be warned… There will be people (or situations) meant to push your limits and test everything you think you've learned on your way to growth.

What's mine?

Over the course of two years, my husband deployed and went on a short tour. We became pregnant with our fifth child with orders to England.

Me and awareness have a love. What is it now? A relationship.

Once I become aware of a way of being that doesn't serve the woman I am becoming in any part of my life, I can no longer ignore it. This awareness guides me to where I need to put more work in. And that is a beautiful thing, but sometimes I'm like, *Ughhh Laniece, why does this cause you to feel this way?* Or, *Why are you reacting this way?* But that phase does not last long because I become excited that there are more opportunities to grow.

Some example questions I have used to help activate my awareness are:

1. Are you holding yourself to unrealistic expectations by constantly looking for flaws or imperfections in yourself?
2. Are you abstaining from certain things because you do not feel you deserve them?

This happens when you cannot enjoy certain things in life because, deep down, you don't feel like you are allowed. Do you pass judgement on others quickly? These judgements are often ones that you place upon yourself as well. From personal experience, these are some of the ways unforgiveness manifested itself in my life. By suppressing my guilt for so long, many of these beliefs and actions became second-nature to me. When you sit back and reflect on how unforgiveness has had a hand in shaping your life, it will amaze you. Then you will begin seeking out more ways to become aware.

Think of awareness as a gift that sometimes comes wrapped in ugly packaging. Yes, becoming aware will give you a sense of enlightenment, but at the same time it can be somewhat overwhelming. When you live a certain way for a long period, and you finally begin to open your eyes and see what's really been going on, it can be hard to comprehend or even slightly traumatic in some ways. But don't allow that to scare you away. Remember, space and grace. You are uncovering and confronting parts of you that you have held on to too long, so naturally there will be discomfort. Still, I challenge you to use those same points of uncomfortableness as points of growth. Yes, this confrontation can be ugly, but the beauty and freedom that lies on the other side is worth it. I promise your work will not be in vain, but you must put in the work.

Listen, there are some pitfalls you might also notice as you become more aware. You may sit back and start to sulk about how you allowed yourself to get to this point or begin to blame others for how you ended up here. If this is you, stop that right now. You are already moving in the direction you want to be by allowing yourself to become aware. From my own experience, **you need to be open to awareness before you can put it into action**. As long as you are in denial, you will never fully be able to tap into the power that lies in being aware. So, from this point, there will be no more blaming or pity parties. If you want to take control of your life, it starts with taking ownership.

You are not powerless. Actually, you're the exact opposite. You are one of the most powerful creatures ever created. Your potential is limitless, and in order to tap into it, you must become aware that it lies within you.

So, what does awareness feel like or look like in real time? Good question.

When you become aware, you start to question your reactions to certain stimuli. It doesn't matter if it makes you angry, sad, happy, or any other emotion. You begin to recognize how active or unactive you are in the story of your life. You will also notice the dynamics of the relationships you have created over time. And in this noticing, you may begin to realize that a lot of your life was built around the negative beliefs you've carried with you up until now.

Carrying unforgiveness has allowed certain people and experiences into your life out of obligation to your guilt.

Becoming aware of the relationship, your inability to forgive yourself, and your current life circumstances are the beginning of your journey toward healing.

I like to think of awareness as awakening. It's refreshing because it allows you to take control of your own life. Once you become intentionally aware, there's no turning back. You have experienced some hard times, and people have tried to break you, but you are still here. Today, I want you to be intentional in your healing process. Becoming aware is one of the most intentional steps in your self-love journey.

Do you remember how perfectly you were created? Before the hurt and the pain? If you don't remember that part of you vividly, please allow yourself to begin acknowledging her, starting now. She deserves your remembrance. I am a strong believer that it is not until we learn who we are that we are able to forgive ourselves. Personally, I had to come face-to-face with the deepest parts of me—the parts of me I perceived to be unforgivable, the parts of me I had been hiding behind a smile and overcompensation. You know, the real stuff. Once I stopped needing to understand the why so much—like *why* did this happen to me, or *why* did it happen that way—I didn't stay in the why stage as long time. But, in order for me to heal, my mindset had to shift.

By acknowledging my guilt and the contempt I felt, I was able to start looking for ways to heal and get past it. Staying in the why state does not allow you to find solutions. If anything, it allows you to continue to wallow in self-pity. I know. I throw the best pity parties. But, at some point, you are at that party alone. It's like no one else feels sorry for you but you.

We like to set up camp in Why Land, right next to Woe is Me River. We've done it for so long that it becomes harder and harder to recognize. But today, we are acknowledging all parts: Guilt, shame, contempt, loneliness, and whatever else you've hidden away. They are no longer allowed to be the elephants in the room.

I don't know why you carry the weight you do. Or even why you may have been unable to forgive yourself. However, I want you to know you are so much more than just deserving. You are worth your own forgiveness a thousand times over. You are allowed to make mistakes, but you will also begin to learn from them. You will begin to apply those lessons to your life when you do.

I know now that perfection is an illusion and something I personally no longer strive for. I endeavor to be better today than I was yesterday. That's it. There is nothing we can do about our past. They have already come, gone and went. And we need to allow ourselves the same grace we extend to others, allowing ourselves the space to practice the lessons learned from our past experiences.

I acknowledge that I want you to take time and figure out what has been holding you in this time warp of unforgiveness. And I want to ask you to ease yourself into grace daily. I know this won't happen overnight, as you may have been holding onto it for years. However, I am proposing that you begin to take off the layers that have built up... The layers that have been blocking you from being who you are designed to be.

You are not defined by your past, and it doesn't have to hold control over your present. Every day, you have the opportunity to make a choice to do and be better. That choice is first made in the mind and then followed by our actions.

chapter 15
Forgiven

> *"To forgive is to set a prisoner free
> and discover that the prisoner was you."*
>
> —LEWIS B. SMEDES

SO WHAT DOES RESPECT HAVE TO DO WITH forgiveness? Everything.

When you respect something, you hold it to the highest regard. It is something or someone you admire. So, when you throw "self" in front of it, that means we are talking about YOU. I believe as you begin to develop your self-respect, you will begin to understand and know your value in a holistic way.

Okay, by now you've realized that you are not perfect. *Whew!* It's a relief to know you can make a mistake. Or, do you?

How many times have you made a mistake and reminded yourself over and over of ways you could have done things better or made statements about how stupid you are? **Stop that right now!** If you continue to remind yourself of what you lack, then you will continue to perpetuate a lacking mindset. In other words, you will continue to believe you are stupid or you lack the ability or resources to accomplish whatever it is you want. Which is a lie straight from the pits.

You have everything you need already stored up inside of you. Think about it like this: You were born completely whole. As time went on, people and society told you who you are and what you can't be. For some of us this was very direct, and for others more indirect; either way, it was done. And each time this happened, you pushed all your gifts deeper inside. You started hiding.

As we grow, we begin to long for different things. Mostly, I believe, we start longing to return back to the feeling of wholeness. I know that much is true for myself. While I cannot assume this is true for others, I do believe many people have a calling to something more, at one point or another, whether they like to admit it or not.

So, how do we go from unforgivable to forgiven? I compare it to baby steps.

We give babies all the time they need to grow and learn to walk and talk. This process is no different. I give myself the same space and grace to learn how to forgive myself and others repeatedly. When I say forgive, I mean it at the deepest level—to truly walk away from something with a clean heart and consciousness.

In everything I do in my life, I have applied the space and grace rule. You will know it's time to implement this rule when you feel guilt, anxiety, or anger. These emotions may arise in your journey because you are not where you think you should be. Just remind yourself you are being born into a new way of thinking, living, and believing. You deserve the space to grow, and you deserve the time it takes to get to a point where you are in control of your reactions.

Forgiveness is one of the many gifts that bring you closer to who you truly are. Don't mix it with continuing to put yourself in the same messed-up situations because you're being "forgiving." This means no going back. It also means that you have acknowledged and accepted whatever has transpired, but it no longer burdens you. You will no longer carry the weight around as a martyr, and you can no longer attend the pity parties thrown in your honor.

Forgiving yourself is not only necessary but essential in your journey to loving yourself to the depths in which you deserve to be loved. It will allow you to handle yourself with more care and give you the grace you need to develop and grow. You deserve your forgiveness. I cannot stress this enough. It is time you get out of your own way because I know you are exhausted from the load you have been carrying, and I am here to tell you that you can put it down right where you are standing.

On this journey of forgiveness and love, there will be things to arise that may impede your progress if you allow it. The biggest thing to remember is that you are changing your "Belief DNA." You are building a new construct where there is still a building. Does that make sense?

Okay, let me explain.

You and I are breaking down the old so you can build the new.

For me, I can struggle with subconscious limiting beliefs. At the beginning of my journey, I did not recognize them. To be honest, it is something I still work on daily, but I am so much more aware of them now. This makes it easier to break them down. When something in my head tells me I am not worthy, I shoot back with all the reasons why I am. Then, I remind myself of all of my great and wonderful attributes. I also remind myself of how I have overcome every obstacle placed before me and thrived.

I wanted perfection for so long. To wake up one day and act like it wasn't something that was a huge part of my belief system would be absurd. Perfection was my drug of choice, and unforgiveness was my high. When I did not achieve the desired flawlessness I once pursued, I punished myself and indulged in a lot of self-pity and other self-destructive behavior I held onto. I could not let anything go when I failed. It was the classic, "Well since I suck, I might as well be the best at that," on repeat. It could get pretty ugly for me, but it was a cycle I was unaware of because it was what I believed to be true: I deserved only "bad" stuff. And because I had accepted these beliefs, when people or situations arose in my life that confirmed what I already believed it cemented my belief a little more.

I need you to re-evaluate the malignant beliefs you hold true about yourself that only continue to tear you down. Sniff out where these beliefs are being reinforced and root them out, one by one. Any environment that fosters negativity in you—whether a group of friends, a podcast, a social media page, post or group you follow—quickly unsubscribe from the idea that you are undeserving, unworthy and forgive yourself.

Unsubscribing is one of many steps to getting back to the real you. Silence the noise. You must be willing to look at the parts of you that are drawn to those areas to begin with. Keep in mind this is not about them. It is about you.

Consider these questions:

1. What are those destructive spaces and places feeding you? (i.e., self-loathing, hatred, guilt, shame)
2. Do they distract you from your own kitchen (meaning your own mess)?
3. What are you getting from them, and why did you seek them out? (i.e., validation)

These are questions that lead to self-discovery, personal development, and ultimately forgiveness. Take the time to journal your answer. You'll be surprised at what comes through and true for you.

This is not the time to pass judgement on what comes up. Just allow it to flow, to be seen, broken down and lived through. This is not a one and done affair either. It is something you get to practice as we continue to evolve and release ways of being that no longer serve who we are becoming.

What limiting belief do you have that you haven't fully acknowledged or even realized yet? Whatever it is, take the time to understand why it is there and if it is holding you back.

There is nothing true about a thought or feeling that puts you in the position of being unworthy or lacking, particularly unable to forgive yourself. Trust me when I say this: We were created whole, every single one of us. This includes you! Do not continue to punish yourself for things you've done in the past. You are still learning and growing, still making mistakes. Allow yourself more space and more grace.

You need this new expansion of space and grace to first understand what it is you believe about you. If someone would have come up to me and said, "Laniece, you won't allow yourself to be happy because you feel damaged and undeserving of anything good," I would have probably tried to slap the taste from their mouth (back then but not now, y'all). No, but seriously, I would have been like, "Who are you talking to? It can't be me." Even though every single word was true.

I would have not been able to receive that message (or forgive) because I did not understand who I was. I was in a place where I had not acknowledged the beliefs that kept me bogged down. So, I was not in the position to be aware, to acknowledge, or to accept anything that questioned the person and beliefs I had held for so long. I am convinced now that we are in a love affair with our negative traits. Some of us are aware of them and choose not to change because "that's just how I am."

As the narrator of your own life, you will be an active component in your new life's trajectory. As you partake in this journey, you will continue to take bold steps toward your transformation. Really taking the time to understand what you believe happiness is for you.

What do you like? What activities do you love participating in that makes your soul smile?

These are questions that will arise during the next season of life, laughter, and love you embark upon, leading you to more discoveries about yourself. I believe understanding where your happiness originates is important. Having this understanding allows you to actively seek out experiences that will bring more joy and peace into your life. This is a part of building your solid foundation because, just as I stated earlier, some of these beliefs still try to arise in my life, and I am sure they will also try to rear their ugly heads in yours as well.

Those negative beliefs will come to try and steal your joy, but they will not be ready for the arsenal you now have in your backpack. So, that is why it is important to build a sturdy foundation so that you are able to STOMP them right out! Allow the new awareness you've begun to build to help you understand what they are and where they come from, and you will not allow them to take up any additional space.

I believe it is important to understand that you are your major roadblock in life. While everyone has contributed to your belief system and current habits, ultimately you have decided to live and accept your life the way it currently is. Forgive yourself for it. The best part about that is you can choose to do something different—right now. When you choose to do something different, you are breaking through your limiting beliefs. You are able to see the truth and value who you are. There may be tears and a wealth of emotions experienced, but you are doing the work that must be done. You are taking the time now to reassess everything in your life. You are reflecting and recognizing where you have been putting your energy and making necessary changes. I know this will become increasingly clearer the more you begin to intentionally look at your life and start letting go of unforgiveness.

chapter 16
It Could Be Your Mother
(Building Intentional Relationships)

"When you truly love yourself, you will be able to give and receive love in a more profound way. Healthy relationships are a reflection of the love and respect you have for yourself."

—LISA NICHOLS

D O YOU HAVE ANY ROADBLOCKS in your life? Is it a person? Is it your mother, sister, brother, and your father's side of the family? While we know THEY don't have all the power, our environment is extremely important. When evaluating relationships in your life, the ones closest to you may be the very ones you need to run from or work on (I'll let you decide).

When we have certain people in our life who perpetuate our negative beliefs, it creates a seemingly perfect storm. You already fundamentally believe certain things about yourself and life in general, so how do we set boundaries and how do we know if a person is only perpetuating the negative beliefs and thoughts we have about ourself?

Here's a quick way to get a sense of what type of person you are dealing with and what they add to your life:

1. Observe your interactions. Is the person constantly uplifting or putting you down?
2. Are they constantly complaining or pointing out how you can do things better?

Those are just quick examples to tell what kind of person you are dealing with, but the most important is to observe. Are you happy in their presence? I am constantly evaluating and re-evaluating the relationships in my life. Not to see how others are serving my purpose but to be in touch with how we are growing together, understanding that some relationships are only here for a season and not forcing anything for a lifetime.

So, if you are struggling with a relationship in your life, it's time you sit back, observe, and reflect—not only their contributions but your own. Remember, we show people how to treat us by how we love (or don't love) ourselves.

Now, you might be thinking, *Does that mean I have to cut everyone off?* No, not in the slightest bit. Actually, I don't want you to do that at all. Isolating yourself will not help you grow. Please hear me when I say that. What you really want is healthy, supportive relationships.

Listen, showing up ready to love openly and being compassionate, showing up and allowing that space and grace for each other to grow is just the first step to working on any relationship. That space and grace must be extended to your friends, family, colleagues, etc. to nourish them in an equally thriving environment—one they also deserve. As you are creating this environment and giving of yourself in the ways you want to receive, the people who are meant to be in your life will be attracted to you.

The point I am trying to make is that when you are more focused on who you are becoming and practicing those things that support your growth, you find less time to worry about people or things that don't align with your current transformation—people I consider roadblocks. By now, you have probably acknowledged that your relationships are a reflection of you, and any perceived *roadblocks* are a result of who you were. Whatever you have allowed to enter and manifest around you has everything to do with you and your choices. The sooner you accept this, the more power you will have over your life and your decisions. So, when evaluating and reflecting, make sure you are starting with yourself and asking why you've allowed things to go so long.

INVITATION:
Co-Creating Healthy Relationships

Let's reflect on the relationships in our lives. Who is most important to you? Once you have those individuals in mind, think about the dynamics of your relationships and answer these questions:

1. How do you feel when you're together?
2. What do conversations consist of?
3. How have you supported one another?
4. Do you cherish the relationship and why?
5. If they no longer were around, how would you feel?
6. Does holding on to this relationship cause more hurt or confusion versus happiness or growth?

I want you to create a list answering these questions and then reflect on anything that comes up about these particular relationships. I believe it's important to understand why certain people are important to us. I also believe it's important to understand what the relationship adds or subtracts to/from our life. Remember, "if a person keeps showing you who they are, take their words and their actions and believe them."

chapter 17
Safety over Softness
(Creating A Secure Life)

> *"Embrace who you are becoming and let go of who you used to be. Your true self is worth celebrating and cultivating."*
>
> —TARANA BURKE

A GIFT USED INAPPROPRIATELY can feel like a curse. A gift received too soon can easily be lost.

Have you ever read stories about people who win the lottery only to be broke within a few years? There is no shortcut to building up your capacity to hold all the beautiful things you want in your life. And we are not just talking about money.

I was gifted with a strong will and personality, but when I didn't know who I was or where I was going, instead of opening doors, I unintentionally blocked them. It wasn't until my late 20s or early 30s that I realized I did not have to be tough; I did not have to build a wall in every relationship or close people out so they didn't let me down.

A term that has recently plagued the internet is "soft woman." A soft woman can broadly be seen as a woman who operates heavily in her feminine nature: Nurturing, intuitive, creative, and gentle. This term has overly simplified the safety that it requires for any woman to feel comfortable in her vulnerability. To be soft is to be safe. *Period.* If a woman is not safe emotionally, physically, or spiritually, more often than not, she will overcompensate to ensure she is safe, and that's when the masculine comments come raining in. In my experience as a Black woman, I have found that we are often portrayed as overly masculine, opinionated, and aggressive. In my case, it didn't help that I had seven brothers; I thought I was a boy up until a certain point. But regardless of your race or socioeconomic status, the environment that cultivates a "soft woman" is a safe one. If you've been fighting your entire life, I wouldn't be surprised if you operate in the world with a certain toughness. But no one wants to be tough all the time; the toughest woman in the room normally could use the biggest hug because they have been fighting and are tired but feel stuck.

To be soft means being vulnerable; it means trusting your environment enough to let your guard down. You may have tried it before and got burned because while you had a desire, you did not co-create the environment that welcomed that side of you. It's kind of like the house was on fire already, and you decided today would be a great day to plant a flower bed. *Umm no*, ma'am. You have to tend to the fire first because whatever you build there will only burn if you don't.

Something I would say often is, "You not gonna have me out here looking like no fool," or "What I look like, Boo Boo the Clown?" These were signals to let you know that I deemed the environment unsafe. Because, there was nothing I loathed more than looking stupid. And I would go to the ends [of the earth] to make sure that never happened. Until the ends got real lonely because of my hypervigilance. Why was it lonely? Because letting people know I was not going to sit around and be played—choosing to be nonchalant and sarcastic over actually connecting and feeling—meant shallow and fleeting relationships. But I was "safe." At least that is what I told myself.

You may be reading this and thinking *'I really desire to be in my soft woman season'*. The only way to begin creating safety around you is by learning what it means to you. Once you know what it means to you, you can begin identifying where its lacking. And next... Yes, there is another step. Next, you can begin communicating your needs and how you would like to begin creating more safety in all areas of your life.

When you don't know how to communicate, you miss out on a lot of healing and lessons. There were many times I chose to remain silent when I should have been speaking up, but I would checkout instead—checkout of that space, out of that conversation, out of that relationship. I had a zero-tolerance mentality, but not in a good way. It was much less about non-negotiables and more about saving or sparing my ego and my perceived safety.

Holding a strong presence is something I learned to love about myself. Just like any gift can be used for "good" or "evil," it can be completely inviting or incredibly isolating. As I have grown, it definitely leans more into the inviting side, but God is still working on me. Personally, I do not aim for a soft life because I want a safe one—safe within myself and my environment.

While I understand my "being safe" starts with me, I refuse to subscribe to the belief that my strong personality or ability to stand for what I believe means I am harsh or brash, meaning hard. Softness is not something I am willing to allow society to define for me, and I hope you don't either.

chapter 18
Loops and Lines (Breaking the Cycles and Setting the Boundaries)

> *"Boundaries are the distance at which I can love you and me simultaneously."*
>
> —NEDRA GLOVER

I RECENTLY READ AN ARTICLE THAT states depression looked different in Black women. I know this because even with all of my education, trainings, and growth it started to sneak up on me, too. As I stalled in life, I stunted my growth. And I could not put my finger on it because it did not look like textbook depression; I just knew something was "off." That is where I opened myself to looking instead of denying that it existed. I get to be honest with how I feel not because I want to hurt others, but because I don't want to keep hurting myself. And this is something I invite you into as well.

Ask yourself, when faced with internal conflict because of a decision of some sort, "Will this decision hurt me?" This can be used when you begin recognizing any people-pleasing tendencies. Not every decision is within your control, but the ones that are, be mindful of why you are choosing (or not) to do something.

I had to understand my loop. What I mean by that is a lot of the feelings and emotions I encountered throughout my life were nothing new. Loneliness and guilt were things that had been recycled and replanted all along. It wasn't hard for me to see the things that were lacking in my life because that was my lens of choice. I choose to see my world as desolate, lacking in love, compassion and forgiveness. At the time, I didn't understand these were choices or that it was my decisions which led me down such a lonely path.

When we begin to recognize our loops and understand them for what they are, that is when we can begin to break them down. For so long, I believed I didn't have a voice, or that what I said didn't matter, but it does. I was born with a voice, and I know it was God's intent for me to use it. However, over the years, I had unknowingly muted myself—not the voice I used to speak with, but the inner voice that was given to me by God. I had started to believe all of the things that were told to me that supported my deficiencies. I walked around as a fraction of the person I was designed to be by choice. And I now know I am not alone in feeling this way.

Perhaps you've been where I've been. Maybe you're stuck there now.

Is that voice calling you to do more still? Or, is it pulling you in a direction you feel you are not ready to go? We often shrug it off as if it's nothing, or we have held mute down for so long the sound is to faint. I am here to help you amplify that voice, the God-given voice He has blessed you with... The voice that guides you in ways that lead to abundance in all aspects of your life.

I have a secret to share. I am not a nice person. I will not act in a pleasing manner so that other people feel comfortable. I am, however, a kind person. I genuinely care about other people and their well-being. To me, being nice is a façade that is put on when you don't want to cause any confrontation or want to present in a certain way that is acceptable. I am just at a point where I am not looking for other people's acceptance, and if you're reading this, you might just be here too. Being nice will have you doing things you don't want to do with people you don't want to do them with or be around.

This is a lesson I had to learn the hard way. Who and how I am may not always be palatable to others, but I will always try my best to be respectful and kind. But I will never water myself down so that my presence is more palatable for *an-y-one*. I've been there and done that. Trying to please everyone will literally suck the life out of you.

I know we've talked about them a little bit in previous chapters, but I really want to break down the importance of not only creating boundaries but enforcing them and re-evaluating them. I feel like when people first hear about boundaries and why they need them, they start throwing them up like giveaways at an Oprah show, "You get a boundary! You get a boundary! Everybody, freeee boundaries!" Now, while I want to commend people who have the courage to begin putting up some boundaries, there has to be a level of intention and commitment behind that boundary, or people will skip right over it and end all back up in your personal space. Boundaries are one of the most important means to creating safety for you to thrive as your authentic self.

Not only that, if you're not careful, those very boundaries you put in place to save you can become your prison. Consider the intention behind the boundary and what it is keeping safe. For example, if you set a boundary against anyone commenting on your relationship, but the relationship is actually unsafe for you, then although you have a boundary, is it serving your highest good? I am no stranger to trying to protect some of my ways of being, but when the urge to protect something that is hurting or hindering me comes up, it is my chance to re-evaluate the boundary I've put into place.

If you can't understand why you have a boundary, it will be difficult for you to explain to someone why they can't cross it. Yup, we're back to it: Communication. Why is this line even drawn in the first place? Maybe it's because you feel like you're being taken advantage of, or there's not enough respect put on your name. Or maybe it's simply because it's not something you feel like doing (it's simply a no). Whatever the reasoning may be, know and understand it for yourself. How did it make you feel when there was no boundary in place? How does it make you feel when that boundary is not honored? By you or someone else? Because if you're over there constantly saying, "Well, I'll do it this once," then you're playing with yourself and everyone else.

There is a struggle that I witness firsthand with the women I work with when first establishing boundaries. They have no issue identifying and naming the boundary needed, and they even build the confidence to begin communicating that boundary. However, when it comes to enforcing it, it's either non-existent or wishy-washy at best. A boundary without enforcement is now an establishment that is open for business. It is an invitation to be consistently used and keeps you out of integrity with yourself. All the work to identify and create the boundary in words means nothing without action.

Once you understand why the boundary is necessary, you must become committed to enforcing it but not so stringent that you don't evaluate its effectiveness or relevance in your life as you evolve. Boundaries aren't permanent structures; they are only as firm and fixed as you allow them to be. What you need at the beginning of this year may not be what you need at the end of this year. Remember, space and grace. You are not married to one way of being. At least I hope you aren't, and neither are your boundaries.

You also are not limited to the type of boundaries you enforce. You have the right to establish emotional, physical, mental, relational, circumstantial (time), material, and any other boundaries you may need in your life. Here are some examples of what those can look and sound like:

- Physical Boundary: "I need some personal space right now, please."
- Emotional Boundary: "I'm not comfortable discussing this topic."
- Mental Boundary: "I respect your opinion, but I have a different perspective."
- Time Boundary: "I can't commit to this project right now; my schedule is full."
- Material Boundary: "I prefer not to lend out my car."
- Relationship Boundary: "I need us to communicate respectfully, even during disagreements."

These are just some examples of what it would look like to communicate healthy boundaries. Understand that they may not be well received, but you must be ready to stand by them. Because a boundary that is communicated but not enforced is just a highlighted entrance to keep disrespecting you.

INVITATION:
Where are Your Boundaries?

WRITE NEDRA GLOVER TAWWAB'S quote at the top of a blank page in your journal: "Boundaries are the distance at which I can love you and me simultaneously." Read the quote several times, letting its meaning sink in.

INITIAL REFLECTION:
- Spend a few minutes reflecting on what this quote means to you personally.
- Consider how it applies to your relationships and self-care practices.

Journaling Prompts

PERSONAL BOUNDARIES:
- Describe a situation where you felt your boundaries were respected. How did it make you feel?

- Recall a time when your boundaries were crossed. What were the consequences, and how did it affect your relationship with that person?

Mutual Respect:
- Think about a relationship where boundaries are well-maintained. How does having clear boundaries enhance the relationship?
- Identify any relationships where boundaries are blurred. How can setting clear boundaries improve these interactions?

Self-Care:
- How do you currently set boundaries to ensure you can take care of yourself?
- List some boundaries you need to establish or strengthen to better love and respect yourself and others.

Identify Key Relationships:
- Write down the names of a few key people in your life (family, friends, colleagues).

ASSESS CURRENT BOUNDARIES:
- For each person, assess the current state of boundaries. Are they clear and respected, or do they need adjustment?

SET OR ADJUST BOUNDARIES:
- Write down specific boundaries you need to set or adjust with each person to ensure mutual respect and self-care. For example:
    - "With my friend, I will limit our calls to once a week to ensure I have time for myself."
    - "In my workplace, I will communicate my limits on working overtime."

COMMITMENT TO CHANGE:
- Choose one boundary you will work on this week. Write a short action plan on how you will implement this boundary and communicate it effectively.
    - Example: "This week, I will tell my coworker that I need to focus on my tasks and can't chat during work hours."

REFLECTION AND FOLLOW-UP:
- At the end of the week, reflect on your experience. Write about any changes you noticed in your feelings, relationships, and overall well-being.
- Adjust your boundaries as needed based on this reflection. Remember, this is your life, and you can choose how you experience it.

chapter 19
Building Self-confidence

"Confidence is the byproduct of making choices that are true to who you are. The more you live authentically, the more confident you become."

—ISSA RAE

WHAT IS THE FIRST THING you think when you see a confident woman? Are you in awe of how she carries herself? Do you feel a bit of jealousy or envy because she is able to move in a way you may desire but don't? Maybe it's a bit of both. I have moved through both sentiments, and I welcome both now if they ever arise. Why would I welcome jealousy or envy? Because I understand that it is just an emotion tied to a belief that ultimately isn't true. My next move would be to get close to her, but not in a creepy way. Close in a way to understand how it is she is able to move so freely. She can become my teacher before I make her my threat.

Stop seeking enemies where God put an alliance. Another woman's greatness is not a reflection of your inadequacies but a reminder of what is possible when you are true to yourself. There is no one or nothing stopping me from moving in the way I desire, except for myself and my beliefs. I know this. And I believe this same statement is true for you.

The moment I began surrounding myself with women who have attributes I want to mirror, I began mirroring them. Proximity is powerful. It can help you discover parts of yourself you never knew. This all boils down to trusting who you are and who you are becoming: *Her.*

Confidence is more than just strutting into a room or speaking on stage in front of thousands of people. Confidence is knowing that the decisions you make are the best decisions for you. It is turning down something good because you know you were designed for something great. Confidence is also holding true to the boundaries that you set, knowing they may cause you to lose some people. It comes from staying true to who you are because you no longer desire to pretend to be someone different. It is quitting that job with those "good benefits" because it's out of alignment. *Now, don't you go quitting your job and saying, "Laniece said this is confidence."* Assess your situation and do what you think is best, but I will share my experience because I sure did quit.

After losing the twins, I had to discover true confidence in myself. Know that when you find something within yourself, you will need to trust and believe a situation will arise to test if you truly are the person you claim to be. My test came in the form of a 5'3" petite blonde-haired, blue-eyed lady. Looking back at it, I see that she is one of my biggest blessings in the form of a lesson.

It was a hot summer day in July 2021, as I prepared for the meeting that would change everything. I had called this meeting with my flight chief to request support as I prepared for my husband to be deployed six months. After losing our twins, I was diagnosed with post-traumatic stress disorder (PTSD) and anxiety. Up until this point, I had been doing what needed to be done to take care of myself and my mental health. I was in such a great space.

I had been working in that particular government position for almost a year. We were stationed in England, and due to the pandemic there was not much opportunity to build a community, which is essential as a military spouse. We had given birth to our last baby in March 2020, and I would be left in a foreign country with three kids, no community, and very little support. But I knew what I needed to make it through the deployment, and physical fitness was at the top of the list. Physical fitness has always been crucial in my healing journey because it is a place where I can be alone, challenge myself, and release.

As a government worker, time can be allocated for physical fitness, but it is up to your supervisor if you can use it or not—a beautiful perk that enticed me to even work there in the first place. I was told it was currently on hold but would be reinstated soon. Almost a year later, I ran in sweating from going to the gym on my lunchbreak. Before this meeting, I had tried for months and jumped through multiple hoops to get this time reinstated, from doctors' notes to getting approval from the civilian personnel office. Nothing, and I mean nothing, would make this woman budge. And I just let it slide. But when the deployment came up, I was like, "Okay, nope."

In this meeting, I asked my flight chief if she would reinstate the physical fitness time we were allotted as employees. I explained why it was important for my mental health and that I would even settle for half of the time. I told her I would not have time to do it in my off time because my husband would be gone, and I would be on double duty mentally, physically, and emotionally. She already knew my story… She knew about the twins. Her response was no. I was heartbroken because I knew this was the end.

Before going into this meeting, I had made a scary decision with the full support of my husband, Darnell. We both agreed that if I could not get what I needed there, I would go all in on my coaching. He has always been my biggest supporter. So, at the end of the meeting, I thanked her for the opportunity and handed in my notice. The rest is history!

This newfound confidence allowed me to go in and ask for what I wanted and to walk away not knowing what I was walking into. My confidence in myself was bolstered by my husband's confidence in me. And to this day, people from that job still tell me how they admire how I was able to stand up for myself and how much it inspired them to do the same in some capacity.

Yes, self-confidence comes from within, but your environment can multiply or diminish it. Seek relationships and spaces that help you to cultivate your confidence because, just like a muscle, it must be practiced. You may never see your full potential if you're not in the right environment, surrounded or supported by the right people, to practice it.

INVITATION:
Shine Bright

THE PURPOSE OF THIS exercise is to provide you with opportunities to develop and strengthen your self-confidence through a variety of activities. It is designed to serve as a starting point in your journey towards building self-assurance. And, as you engage in this process, you will uncover and explore new strategies and approaches to boost your confidence in different aspects of your life.

SET THE SCENE:
- Choose a vibrant, uplifting environment where you feel energized. This could be a sunny outdoor space, a brightly lit room, or a favorite cozy corner at home.
- Play your favorite upbeat music in the background to set a positive mood.

Dance Party:

- Create a playlist of your favorite empowering songs.
- Dance like nobody's watching! Let loose, have fun, and allow yourself to feel the music. Moving your body energetically can uplift your mood and boost your confidence.
- If you're comfortable, record a short video of yourself dancing and watch it back, celebrating your freedom and joy.

Compliment Circle (with Friends):

- Gather a small group of supportive friends (in-person or virtually).
- Take turns giving and receiving genuine compliments. Each person should share one thing they admire about others in the group.
- Reflect on the compliments you receive and write them down in your notebook/journal. Notice how it feels to hear positive feedback from those who care about you.

EMPOWERMENT PHOTOSHOOT:
- Dress in an outfit that makes you feel powerful and confident.
- Set up a mini photoshoot. Use your phone or camera to take a series of photos where you pose confidently.
- Choose your favorite photos and create a visual confidence board. Place it somewhere you'll see it often as a reminder of your powerful self.
- Smile at yourself and appreciate your own presence.

CELEBRATE ACHIEVEMENTS:
- Create a list of your achievements and milestones, no matter how big or small.
- Plan a mini celebration for yourself. This could be a special treat, a fun outing, or a relaxing spa day at home. Acknowledge and reward your progress.

ADVENTURE CHALLENGE:
- Identify an activity that excites you but is slightly outside of your comfort zone

(e.g., taking a dance class, joining a public speaking group, or trying a new sport).
- Commit to doing this activity within the next week. Journal about your experience and how it made you feel more confident.

GRATITUDE AND REFLECTION:
- End your exercise by sitting quietly with your journal.
- Write down three things you are grateful for and three things you love about yourself.
- Reflect on how these positive aspects contribute to your self-confidence and overall happiness.

chapter 20
Awareness

"When you stop growing, you start dying."
—WILLIAM S. BURROUGHS

AWARENESS IS SOMETHING I believe we were born with. As I watched my son grow over this past year, I noticed how keenly aware he is of his surroundings. Anything he felt, he expressed. He did not care if you liked his crying; when he wanted or needed something, he communicated it the only way he knows how: He wept. He was aware of what he needed and did not seek permission to ask for it.

As we have grown throughout life, we are taught what is appropriate to express and how we are supposed to behave. We are groomed to become socially acceptable in everyone's eyes but our own.

Self-awareness is the ability to recognize your own thoughts, feelings, behaviors, and tendencies. To be self-aware is to know where you're absolutely that chick and where you're falling short. It allows you to develop relationships that are not ruled by your emotions.

My realization of my previous inability to forgive and love myself led to my recognition of where those beliefs' impacts had shown throughout my entire life. It showed me where I was operating as a fearful mother, who felt I could never parent my daughter the way she needed to be raised because I was not competent enough. It glared its light on the fact that I was in and out of being an emotionally detached wife, because I didn't know how to love my husband. In reality, at that time, I didn't know how to love myself, so loving him how I wanted to love him wasn't even an option I had access to.

Self-awareness helps you move from seeking to speak to be understood to learning to sit back and really listen. It can move you from fighting for your limitations to accepting your infinite nature. Once I became aware, I could acknowledge that it was me who had created this false narrative about my ability to love myself and those around me. I could release it back into the nothingness from which it came.

Say it with me, "Every situation in my life is a direct reflection of who I am." This is not the easiest truth to come around to, but it is one of the most powerful awakenings you can have. By accepting that it was me who needed to do the work, I became focused on learning what it meant to love me. I began to figure out why I felt the way I did. It was through these trials that I learned the terms space and grace. Everything helped me to come to the realization that it truly could only get better from here.

If you are trying to be cute while becoming more self-aware and growing, choose a different path. This is not for the cute and dainty; it's ugly over here and requires a lot of heavy lifting. You will get in the thick of it and feel like you're surrounded by mess. You will learn that embarrassment is a part of the process, and egos die slow deaths. With practice, you will laugh at what once made you feel embarrassed or triggered, and you will do it over and over again because that is what happens when you grow. You can't be obsessed with how your growth looks to the outside world.

After losing the twins, I became fed up with learning through hurt and pain. Something had to give. I wanted to learn through the wisdom of past mistakes and through wisdom passed down by generations. The show I had been putting on for everyone else was not worth my life, and it sucks that it took such a huge trauma to happen in my life to wake me up. Sometimes, I think my babies were sent here to save me—to teach me. They had to have known I was on the path of self-destruction, and they would not allow it. Choosing this belief brings me peace.

We live in an instant society. Many people want growth now but not the work that comes with it. They want riches and stability without investing and taking the time to build a firm foundation. What I want you to understand is whatever it is you want, you must first prepare for. Dig your ditches. Get ready for the increase of abundance in your life by becoming the person who can receive it.

This is an odyssey.

Your journey will continue until you leave this earth. This will require awareness, faith, and confidence in who you are and who you were called to become.

chapter 21
Choose to Be Seen

"You may not control all the events that happen to you, but you can decide not to be reduced by them."

—MAYA ANGELOU

I CAN REMEMBER being on the playground, lining up for a game of dodgeball and screaming from the inside, "Pick me. Pick me." Those same screams followed me throughout my life. Pick me because I deserve to be noticed, don't I? There was a constant battle between believing I was worthy or deserving. This story is not only true for me, but it is a living truth for many.

The person staring back at you in the proverbial mirror of life is your forever project—your lifelong friend, your confidant. They deserve your full love and attention. Being unseen by the world or feeling like no one understands, or maybe that no one values you, is a reflection of how you feel about yourself. You may have not recognized this but take the time to assess it now.

When you think of who you are, do you immediately think of what you lack? If your mind entertains any of these thoughts, when you believe you are inadequate, that can become a painful place to operate from.

This is an internal battle many people often fail to realize they are doing. It's like being on autopilot and surrendering to the less-than-optimal reality you've created for yourself. But if you are reading this, you are beginning to wake up. You are now recognizing that you are your most valuable asset and that if you do not love and care for yourself, you will never understand what your happy looks and feels like. So, it is time to see you for the amazing person you are!

I listened to a podcast with my husband one day, and the show spoke about what it takes to be able to see. I cannot quote it verbatim, but I do remember there being two things needed to see: Eyes and light. Without one or the other, you will see nothing. How true that is!

When you dim your light and take up residence in the shadows, you are choosing to remain unseen. Having eyes does not automatically mean sight. It's coupling your sense of awareness with your internal light that leads to vision and makes all things possible. However, when we constantly choose to remain hidden, when we choose to dim that inner light, we become blind not only to the light within but also to the light that is the world. It is hard to see the good in anything when you can't even see the good in yourself.

From this day forward, I am personally challenging you to see you for who you are in this moment. See who you are and learn how to love yourself in ways you never thought possible. And through that love, allow the transformation to take place—allow the healing.

What exactly does it mean to be seen? To be unafraid?

It means you are no longer scared of you—your past life or your past failures. You are no longer afraid of who you've become and the mistakes you have made. You begin to see that you deserve the same space and grace you have afforded everyone else, the luxury of knowing your worth and your truth.

I didn't love myself, and I mean that in the most literal physical, spiritual, and emotional way. As I reflect on the moments where I know I deserved my love the most, I clearly see that I chose to withhold it because I honestly did not know how to do anything else. It became easy to avoid loving and taking care of me because self-neglect became a daily practice. I didn't know what loving me looked like, and I definitely didn't know what it felt like. So, for me, it was the "you can't miss what you never had" syndrome. It was the lie I chose to believe that I didn't deserve it even if I knew what it was.

I read or heard somewhere that you can either learn through wisdom or trauma. And after experiencing all that I have in this life, I can say with certainty that statement is absolutely true. In the interest of being vulnerable, I think it has been important for me to share this story of loss with you because I have gained so much more by doing so. While not loving yourself is a choice, choosing to do so can happen slowly over time. It's the small decisions we make that continue to perpetuate the self-loathing reality that gets experienced daily. Do not let that become your default setting, your normal routine. Shake it up! Start questioning why you feel or are allowing certain experiences. Understand that doubt may try to seep in, or you may become concerned with how people might view your journey, but you cannot allow that to hold you back.

When you love yourself, you become open to new opportunities and experiences that will happen organically, as love allows us to live outside of the confines we once created for ourselves—to be seen. In order to get to back to this place, we must begin undoing all the things that have kept us bound, primarily limiting beliefs.

What scares you most? Is it the unknown of the whole process? Is it the fear that you can't accomplish what you set out to do? Whatever the fear you feel, it isn't true. Well, it is only as true as you believe it to be.

On the path to self-discovery, things will arise and others may not work out as you intended, but they are always working out for you, remember? In every lesson, there is an opportunity to apply it and to become better. If you have been repeating these lessons and never learning from them, that is the scariest part. You could literally die without ever realizing this or without living the life you were created for. If that doesn't make you want to try something different, then let this be the gentle nudge that reminds you tomorrow isn't guaranteed.

Some people have very specific ideas while others seem unsure of what living looks like for them. I can promise any negative beliefs, thoughts, or feelings you have—anything that makes you want to buckle and break or run and hide—are just that. Negative. It's not what is intended for you, no matter where you are on the spectrum.

My one final piece of advice?

Move towards the things that make you feel good. Not those temporary fixes (i.e., impulses or indulgences that are more destructive than a distraction), but those things that are good sources of joy—the things that make your soul smile. I believe you know the difference, and I trust you will honor those parts of you that align with doing, being, living, and feeling well.

epilogue

LISTEN, LIFE IS NOT ABOUT PERFECTION. It is about progression. And your progression is unique to you, just like your happiness and everything else that brings you joy. In the case of the sunflower, I finally figured out how to deal with the root of my issues. A new fancy pot was necessary but what was critical was being planted in fresh soil. Recognizing this was a crucial point in my evolution journey.

Self-love is a term in today's world that feels overused. In reality, it's simply *under*practiced and misunderstood… And saturated by what society wants to highlight. Being able to practice self-love starts with first developing a relationship with you. It is not just about vacations and pedicures. Yes, all those self-care practices are great. But there can be no light without shadow. So, let's not subscribe to shallow mindedness. This reeks of rotted roots, dry dirt and a cracked flowerpot.

Be willing to look at and to understand the hard stuff. You must make decisions that align with your values, and if you don't know what those are create them. Start from a space of understanding and nurturing your own value as a God-given beautiful creature of this life. Create values from a knowingness that nothing in this world will ever give you what you are worth and let that be okay. It does not mean you should settle.

Do you desire passion? Excitement? Or, quiet and calm?

Maybe you desire both-and in different seasons. That is fine. Just be open to communicating it to the people who love you (and the people I pray you love). I open space for my desires to be met, and I also open space for others to communicate theirs as well.

My mentor, Preston Smiles, says all the time that "we cannot take people where we ourselves are not willing to go." He had put to words what I already felt in my heart, and I think you know it too. Your current situation will not magically change. Be very intentional and trust you can do it. By *it* I mean embracing all parts of you, including turning and facing the parts you may have demonized, the parts of you that remind you of any abuse, of abortions of any kind (i.e., dreams you've given up on, relationships you've inappropriately handled, self-neglect, and any other things you may need to practice forgiving yourself for). There's still time to be who you want to be—who you are destined to become.

My pain is no longer a dark cloud over my life. This sunflower is rooted in self-love, grounded in truth, and standing tall. The traumas of my life propelled me into a masterfully crafted purpose that now includes you. How do you know when you have found yours? How do you know when you are back on track to becoming who were intended to be?

This happens when the uncomfortable is no longer uncomfortable.

When outgrowing your old life yields a new one.

When the trauma isn't a reminder of where you've been but where it's brought you.

When you're well on your way to *Becoming Her!*

author's note

I WANT TO START WITH A THANK YOU TO God who kept me. The biggest thank you to my husband Darnell, who has loved and supported me along my odyssey. Thank you for loving me while I was learning to love myself. Thank you for ALWAYS believing I could through your words and actions. Our love story will always be my favorite. I want to also thank my children Kennedy, Darius, and Lennox, and the twins, who have watched and loved me as I continuously evolve. A relationship outside of oneself can never be truly fulfilling if you don't know who you are within. A special thanks to my sister Fanisha and my sisterhood for believing in me and supporting me always. Thank you to my brothers, for always speaking life into me, my baby brother Ephraim for waking up to listen to me read parts of the book to him.

To my parents, Michael and Carrie, two very loving people who had a lot on their plates... I know it was not easy raising nine children and having to divide your time between each of us had to be equally difficult. Still, you did it with ease. In my eyes, you did an amazing job—especially, Mommy. Thank you for bending over backwards for us. You guys showed me what unconditional love looks like through your celebrations and tribulations. You taught me the power of joy! Thank you to my favorite Aunt Jackie who showed and taught me at a young age what it looks like to be in service to other people.

I want to thank Little Laniece (aka Mooches) for always reminding me to shine. A huge thank you to my editor Shaundale, who helped me birth my first book baby!

For the reader, yes you, thank you for sharing your odyssey with me. May you now create the space and grace you need in the time you now have to give yourself. It's time to start again. You can do it, and you must do it now.

www.ingramcontent.com/pod-product-compliance
Lightning Source LLC
Chambersburg PA
CBHW071505180426
43194CB00052B/2279